And ye shall hear of wars and rumours of war;
see that ye be not troubled, for all these
things must come to pass, but the end is not yet.
Matthew 24:6

NIMBUS PUBLISHING LIMITED

THE
BLACK
BATTALION
——— 1916-1920 ———
CANADA'S BEST KEPT
MILITARY SECRET

CALVIN W. RUCK

Nimbus Publishing Limited
P.O. Box 9301, Station A
Halifax, N.S.   B3K 5N5

(A previous version was published under ISBN 0-921201-00-1: *Canada's Black Battalion: No. 2 Construction, 1916-1920*, The Society for the Protection and Preservation of Black Culture in Nova Scotia.)

Canadian Cataloguing in Publication Data

Ruck, Calvin W. (Calvin Woodrow), 1925-
  Canada's black battalion

Rev. ed.
Bibliography: p.
Includes index.
ISBN 0-920852-92-0

1. Canada. Canadian Army. Construction battalion, 2 - History. 2. World War, 1914-1918 - Regimental histories - Canada. 3. World War, 1914-1918 - Blacks - Canada. 4. Blacks - Canada - History - 20th century. 5. World War, 1914-1918 - Canada. I. Title.

UC90.R82 1987   940.4'12'71   C87-094667-6

Design: Kathy Kaulbach
Typesetting: Mandala Electronic Publishing, Dartmouth, N.S.
Printing and Binding: Seaboard Printing Ltd., Halifax, N.S.

Printed and bound in Canada

Title-page photo: Company A, No. 2 Construction Battalion, CEF

Grateful acknowledgement is made to the following sources for permission to reprint:

Public Archives of Canada; Public Archives of Nova Scotia; NC Press for an extract from *Shadd: The Life and Times of Mary Shadd Cary*; Robin Winks, *The Blacks in Canada: A History* (Yale University Press); Leo W. Bertley for extracts and reproductions from *Canada and Its People of African Descent*; Ernest Green, "Upper Canada's Black Defenders," *Papers and Records of the Ontario Historical Society*, 27: 1931; Dorothy Sterling for extracts from *The Making of an Afro-American: Martin Robison Delany* (Doubleday); Headley Tullock and NC Press for extracts from *Black Canadians: A Long Line of Fighters*; University of Toronto Press (The Champlain Society, 1977) and Barbara Wilson for excerpts from *Ontario and the First World War, 1914-1918*; McClelland and Stewart and Pierre Berton for an excerpt from *The Promised Land: Settling the West, 1896-1914*; Colin A. Thomson for a photo from *Blacks in Deep Snow: Black Pioneers in Canada* (J. M. Dent & Sons); Truro *Daily News* for an article on Jeremiah (Jerry) Jones. The author apologizes for any inadvertent omissions.

To the memory of all Blacks
who served in
the Great War,
1914-1918

CONTENTS

FOREWORD

On Remembrance Day in 1985, when I composed the foreword for the first edition of this memorial to the No. 2 Construction Battalion, CEF, I noted that the spirit of the Battalion was still alive in Atlantic Canada. Through the initiative of the Black Cultural Centre, Dartmouth, the Black communities of Nova Scotia had organized the Reunion and Recognition Weekend of November 1982 and encouraged Mr. Ruck to document the part the Battalion played in the Great War.

With this second tribute, only a few tangible memories of our country's military coming of age at Vimy Ridge remain—as both our witness and our touchstone—seventy years after the guns have been stilled. Many of the old comrades—the true comradeship formed in the desperation of war—have gone. In only a handful of years, we will never learn more of the "war to end all wars." Canadians, British, Germans, Tonkinese, Americans, French, Turks . . . they will all be gone; there will be no more veterans of that epic conflict. Only from men such as William Carter, A. Seymour Tyler and Gordon Charles Wilson will we know those years; from these men we must learn to remember.

Bruce F. Ellis, Curator
The Army Museum, Halifax Citadel
Halifax, N.S.
September 1, 1987

PREFACE

This book is not intended to be a major, detailed historical work on Black veterans in the Great War (1914-18). In truth, it developed out of a reunion-and-recognition weekend sponsored by The Society for the Protection and Preservation of Black Culture in Nova Scotia (also known as the Black Cultural Society) to honour, and pay tribute to, the forgotten, unknown and unsung Black veterans of World War I.

Any historical accounts are essentially brief overviews of Black military involvement. It is hoped, however, that this book will serve a number of positive, practical purposes: commemorate, and pay lasting tribute to, all the Black Canadians who faithfully served King and Country in the Great War; create a much greater awareness and appreciation of the fact that Black Canadians played a role in that war, which led to the recognition of Canada as a sovereign nation; point out the attitudes and obstacles that Blacks had to overcome in order to participate in the defence of their country; and chronicle and preserve the reunion-and-recognition events held in November 1982 for veterans of the No. 2 Construction Battalion, CEF, and other units.

The Black military heritage in Canada is still generally unknown and unwritten. Many Canadians of all races have no idea that Blacks served, fought, bled and died on European battlefields, all in the name of freedom. The fact that approximately six hundred Black soldiers served in a segregated non-combatant labour battalion during World War I has been one of the best kept secrets in Canadian military history.

The story of the overt racist treatment of Black volunteers is a shameful chapter in the history of this country. It does, however, represent an important part of the Black legacy and the Black experience.

Lest we forget.
Calvin W. Ruck, RSW
September 8, 1987

INTRODUCTION

Black Canadians have a long and honourable tradition of patriotism, sacrifice and heroism in the British and Canadian Armed Forces. From the American Revolution (1775-83) to the Korean War (1950-53), Blacks fought, bled and died on behalf of Empire, King and Country.

During the American Revolution, the Crown encouraged slaves to desert their rebel masters and join the British lines. Thousands responded to the call and the opportunity to escape the shackles of slavery. Many former slaves worked as labourers for the British, while others served in combat units. One corps, the Black Pioneers, served faithfully throughout the war and received commendations for bravery and conduct.

Following the end of the Revolution in 1783, members of the Black Pioneers, as well as other Black veterans, joined the exodus of United Empire Loyalists to the Maritimes and Upper Canada. C. Bruce Ferguson's study of Black settlements in Nova Scotia referred directly to the military service of Blacks in British army units during the Revolution:

Among the Negroes who came to Nova Scotia with the Loyalists were a considerable number of freed men as well as slaves. Most of the freed men had escaped from their masters in the Southern Colonies.

One Negro Corps had rendered military service on the side of the British and nearly every Loyalist Corps had representatives of the African race in its ranks as buglers, musicians or pioneers. British generals had offered protection to such slaves who sought refuge within their lines.

A large number of these were brought to Birchtown near Shelburne where they received lands, and for at least three years, rations were distributed to them by the British Government. Other freed Blacks were similarly settled at Preston, Digby, St. John [sic] or some adjacent point.[1]

Black Loyalists who had served in the British Forces also settled in Upper Canada. They made their way from the United States to the Windsor and Niagara Falls areas after the war. In *Black Canadians*, Headley Tullock wrote, "Scattered among mili-

William Edward Hall, VC

tary records, correspondence and records of land grants are references to Black soldiers who fought alongside the British and who were now coming north to claim the land promised."[2]

Today, a monument on Wellington Street in Toronto, Ont., commemorates those who fought in the War of 1812. In that war, Blacks helped defend Upper Canada against American invaders. According to Tullock, a number of volunteers in Niagara were organized into the Company of Coloured Men:

Black settlers had always been in the regular militia along the Niagara frontier. When war was declared, Richard Pierpoint, who had served in Butler's Rangers in the American Revolution, proposed the formation of a special company of Blacks.

The Company of Coloured Men was formed under the leadership of a white man, Capt. Robert Runchey. Some Blacks transferred specially to this company although the majority were dispersed throughout the army.[3]

Black soldiers served in a number of non-segregated units, such as the Glengarry Light Infantry and the 104th Regiment of Foot (New Brunswick). They saw action in several famous engagements, including Queenston Heights, Lundy's Lane, Niagara Town, Fort George and Stoney Creek. Wrote Tullock:

At Queenston Heights, October 13, 1812, the Company of Coloured Men was part of the reinforcements that arrived with Colonel Sheaffe and saved the day for the Canadians.

General Brock had been killed and the Americans commanded the Heights. Sheaffe and his men, approaching from the rear, charged and broke through the American defence tumbling some men over the escarpment to the rocks below and scattering the rest to be pursued by the Indian Scouts. The Americans surrendered, Queenston was saved.[4]

Many of the Black soldiers in the War of 1812 were former slaves who had escaped to Upper Canada in search of freedom and protection under the British flag. It is a historical irony that the runaways had in reality sought refuge in a society that did not legally abolish slavery until 1833.

Black militia units played a major role in quelling the Upper Canada Rebellion (1837-39) as well. Prior to 1837, the majority of militia units had no Blacks in their ranks. With the outbreak of the Rebellion, led by William Lyon Mackenzie, the Government welcomed Black participation. As Tullock pointed out, Black units were raised in a number of towns and villages, including Niagara, Chatham, Amherstburg, Hamilton and Windsor:

Nearly a thousand volunteered for service after the Patriots were defeated in the Battle of Toronto in December, 1837. On every front in Western Ontario, Blacks were an important part of the British forces. In all, five companies of Black soldiers (still under white officers!) took part in some of the most important and exciting incidents of the war.[5]

At the time, Sir Francis Bond Head, the Lieutenant-Governor of Upper Canada, commended Black loyalty to Britain:

When our Coloured population were informed that American citizens had taken violent possession of Navy Island for the double object of liberating them from the domination of British rule and of imparting to them the blessings of republican institutions, based upon the principle that all men are born equal, did our Coloured brethren hail their approach. No!

On the contrary they hastened as volunteers in wagon loads to the Niagara frontier to beg from me permission that in the intended attack upon Navy Island they might be permitted to form the forlorn hope — in short they supplicated that they might be allowed to be foremost to defend the glorious institutions of Great Britain.[6]

By the 1850s, Blacks began receiving military honours for their bravery. One of the first Canadians to win the Empire's highest award for valour, the Victoria Cross, was William Edward Hall, a Black seaman from Horton's Bluff, N.S. He was the son of former slaves who had been rescued by a British warship during the War of 1812.

During the Indian Mutiny against the British, while serving as "Captain of the Foretop" on the HMS *Shannon*, Hall participated in the relief of Lucknow, India, on November 16, 1857. In fact, his heroic action was largely responsible for the city's liberation.

One of the 410 seamen and marines selected to travel overland to Cawnpore and Lucknow, Hall volunteered to join a gun crew sent to relieve Lucknow's garrison. The crew's members were killed one by one until only Hall and a badly wounded lieutenant remained alive. With complete disregard for his own safety, he continued to fire the gun until the wall was breached, allowing the relief force to enter the city. His performance, which also gained him the Indian Mutiny Medal, has been described by one writer as "almost unexampled in war."[7]

Hall had previously fought in the Crimean War, distinguishing himself in 1854 and 1855 at the siege of Sebastopol. During that campaign, he won the Turkish Crimean War Medal and the British Crimean War Medal.

In 1860, prior to the American Civil War, approximately six hundred Blacks emigrated from California to Canada to escape racial persecution. They settled on the colony of Vancouver Island. The Blacks were not popular with the local residents, and after being denied the right to join the volunteer fire brigade, they decided to organize a volunteer military force. In April of that year, the Governor of the colony, Sir James Douglas, gave the necessary authority to proceed with recruiting. The Black force was the first troop in the history of British Columbia and was officially known as the Victoria Pioneer Rifle Corps. One writer, J. S. Matthews, presented a rather picturesque description of the unit:

"This corps is composed wholly of coloured persons, most of whom are naturalized British subjects, immigrants from the United States," states a return of "Militia, Volunteers, etc.," August 1st, 1862, and signed by James Douglas, afterwards Sir James, first Governor of the Crown Colony of British Columbia. It informs us that the "Victoria Pioneer Rifle Corps" consisted of one captain, two lieutenants, and forty privates, no horses, no artillery; was organized in April 1860; and is drilled twice a week. The "African Rifles"—it was thus nicknamed, for every member was a full-blooded negro—can rightfully claim to have been the first officially authorized military force in Western Canada. Truth is frequently stranger than fiction.[8]

Meanwhile, other Black Canadians were playing a major role in the American Civil War (1861-65), a conflict in which the inhuman institution of slavery was a key issue. A large number of Blacks, including many former slaves, crossed the border to fight for the Union Army against the slave-holding states of the South. They served primarily in combat regiments raised in Massachusetts, New York and Michigan.

Major Martin Robison Delany, United
States Army, Civil War (1861-65), was the
first Black commissioned officer in the
United States Armed Forces. He resided
in Chatham, Ont., prior to the Civil War.

One of the key players in the recruitment process was a Black-
American expatriate from Virginia, Martin Robison Delany. He
was residing in Chatham, Ont., prior to the outbreak of the
Civil War, and he became the first Black commissioned officer in
United States history. Delany's contribution to the Union cause
was the recruitment of thousands of Blacks into the Army. In a
private audience with President Abraham Lincoln, he put forth a
unique proposal:

*I propose, sir, an army of Blacks, commanded by Black officers. This
army to penetrate the heart of the South, with the banner of Emancipation
unfurled, proclaiming freedom as they go. By arming the emancipated,
taking them as fresh troops, we could soon have an army of 40,000 Blacks
in motion. It would be an irresistible force.*[9]

President Lincoln accepted the radical proposal, and he asked
Delany to command the unit. "On February 26, 1865," wrote historian Dorothy Sterling, "Secretary of War Edwin Stanton signed
the document that transformed Martin R. Delany, free Black, into
a Major in the United States Army."[10]

Delany was instrumental in securing the services of a Black

woman, Mary Shadd Cary, also of Chatham, to accelerate the recruitment of Black Canadians. She is believed to have been the only woman commissioned as a recruiting officer during the American Civil War.[11]

Decades later, during the South African Boer War (1899-1902), a small number of Blacks served with the Canadian contingent. The phrase "white man's war" is believed to have originated during that conflict: both the British and the Boers displayed a reluctance to use Black Africans as front-line combat troops.[12]

At the outbreak of World War I in 1914, Black Canadians were also caught up in the patriotic fervour of this conflict, which was being hailed as "the war to end all wars," "a war to make the world safe for democracy." A large number of Blacks who volunteered for the Canadian Expeditionary Force (CEF) became painfully aware, however, of the concept of "a white man's war" in 1914, as recruiting stations from Nova Scotia to British Columbia turned them away.

Black leaders and individuals throughout the country protested the exclusion of Black volunteers. In Ontario, one Black leader, J. R. B. Whitney, offered to recruit and raise a Black platoon, but no authorized battalion would accept one.[13] In response to the mounting Black protest and as a compromise solution to the dilemma, the Chief of the General Staff in Ottawa, Major-General W. G. Gwatkin, proposed the formation of one or more Black labour battalions.[14]

The outcome of Gwatkin's proposal was the formation in 1916 of the No. 2 Construction Battalion, CEF. The unit was made up of recruits from across the country, as well as the United States. After receiving training at Pictou and Truro, N.S., the Battalion left Halifax, N.S., in March 1917 for overseas service.

More than sixty-five years later, The Society for the Protection and Preservation of Black Culture in Nova Scotia honoured those Blacks who fought in World War I. During the Remembrance Day weekend of November 1982, World War I veterans, comprising survivors of the No. 2 Construction Battalion, several other army units and the Merchant Navy, gathered at a historic reunion banquet.

CHAPTER
N⁰ 1

THE REJECTION
OF BLACK VOLUNTEERS

For more than a century, Black Canadians have unquestionably demonstrated their loyalty by volunteering for military service. In August 1914, however, when World War I erupted, Black Canadians were treated like third-class citizens. The message that they would not be included in the patriotic and military institutions of Canada came across loud and clear.

After the War broke out, Canadians flocked to the recruiting stations, and in October 1914, the first contingent of troops sailed from Quebec City for England and the battlefields of Belgium and France. Historian Robin Winks reported that a few Blacks were included in that vanguard:

Two months after the outbreak of war the first contingent of Canadian troops arrived in Britain. An initial call for volunteers was expanded to a quarter of a million in 1915 and to half a million in 1916, most of whom were sent to the Western Front. A few Negroes were among these troops, for individual Blacks were permitted to enlist in such local regiments as would accept them.[1]

Throughout the country, from Nova Scotia to British Columbia, large numbers of Black volunteers were being rejected strictly on the basis of race or colour. Officials at some recruiting stations bluntly told Black volunteers that it was "a white man's war." In other instances, they said, more tactfully, "We will call you when we need you." In western Nova Scotia, Blacks often heard, "We do not want a chequer-board army."[2]

Black people in a number of provinces viewed military service in wartime not only as a right, but a responsibility. They were not prepared to accept meekly a policy, official or unofficial, that rejected them on racial grounds. A struggle for basic human rights was beginning to take shape.

Several Black leaders and some white supporters in various parts of the country began to question, and seek clarification on, recruiting policies and practices. They directed their concerns and inquiries to the highest levels of both the civilian and military authorities.

One of the earliest recorded acts of protest came from Arthur Alexander, a Black leader in Buxton, Ont. Four months after the War started, he wrote a letter to the Minister of Militia and Defence, Sir Sam Hughes. Essentially, Alexander asked why Black men were not allowed to enlist in the Canadian Expeditionary Force (CEF). The reply he received raised more questions than answers. As military historian Barbara Wilson wrote:

It was evident in 1914, however, that Negro volunteers were not welcome in the Canadian Expeditionary Force, and Arthur Alexander of Buxton asked the Department of Militia for an explanation. He was told that the selection is entirely in the hands of commanding officers and their selections or rejections are not interfered with from headquarters.

Mr. Alexander did not pursue the matter, but it was taken up less than a year later by George Morton of Hamilton, who in essence received the same reply.[3]

Morton's letter to the Minister, dated September 7, 1915, explicitly outlined the existing unacceptable situation:

The reason for drawing your attention to this matter, and directly leading to the request for this information, is the fact that a number of Colored men in this city (Hamilton) who have offered for enlistment and service have been turned down and refused solely on the grounds of color or complexional distinction, this being the reason given on the rejection or refusal card issued by the recruiting officer.

As humble, but loyal, subjects of the King trying to work out their own destiny, they think they should be permitted in common with other peoples to perform their part and do their share in this great conflict.

So our people, gratefully remembering their obligations in this respect, are most anxious to serve their King and Country in this critical crisis in its history, and they do not think they should be prevented from so doing on the ground of the hue of their skin.[4]

The letter reached Hughes by way of T. J. Stewart, the Member of Parliament for Hamilton, Ont. Hughes, evidently, turned the letter over to the Acting Adjutant-General, Brigadier-General W. E. Hodgins, who replied:

There are no regulations or restrictions which prohibit or discriminate against the enlistment and enrollment of coloured men who possess the necessary qualifications.

The final approval of any man, regardless of colour or other distinction, must of course rest with the officer commanding the particular unit which the man in question is desirous of joining.[5]

From Westville, N.S., Captain J. F. Tupper wrote to Hughes informing him that more than one hundred Blacks had been rejected by the Army. He volunteered to try and recruit a thousand

Black and white people to form a regiment:

As I have unsolicited applications from over one hundred colored men wishing to enlist and none of the regiments being formed will take them, if I secure the names of a thousand men, white and colored, willing to enlist in a regiment to consist of white and colored men, will you accept them as a new Nova Scotia regiment?

It is felt that the colored men should be allowed to go, but the regiments being formed do not want them.[6]

Tupper's proposal was rather radical considering the prevailing atmosphere, and there is no evidence available to suggest that his offer received serious consideration.

In Ottawa, an inquiry from Fleming B. McCurdy, the Member of Parliament for Colchester, Ont., to Prime Minister Robert Borden was referred to the Chief of the General Staff for a reply. Major-General W. G. Gwatkin responded that the Minister of Militia and Defence was not in favour of raising a Black regiment. He added, "In the last extremity we might organize a company or two. But would Canadian Negroes make good fighting men? I do not think so."[7]

In New Brunswick, twenty Black volunteers persistently tried to enlist and were finally accepted into the Army. On November 15, 1915, however, when they reported to the military camp at Sussex, they were not permitted to join the 104th Battalion, CEF. Instead, they were sent back to Saint John.

The reality of twenty fit, enlisted and unwanted Black soldiers in New Brunswick created a furore that resounded in Ottawa and unfolded across the nation. On November 18, Lieutenant-Colonel Beverley R. Armstrong of Saint John sent a telegram to the Secretary of the Militia Council in Ottawa asking if a Black battalion was being formed in any part of Canada. With a tone of urgency, he indicated that "twenty colored men here have passed medical examination and are anxious to go."[8]

After the men were sent back to Saint John, a resident of that city, John T. Richards, wrote to Sir Sam Hughes seeking his intervention and describing the reception extended to Black soldiers at Camp Sussex:

On arrival they met the 2nd Commanding Officer who told them he knew nothing of their coming, and to get right away from there as he would not have them at all, in fact insulted them. He told them that a Colored Battalion was being formed in Ontario and to go there.[9]

Richards informed Hughes that some of the soldiers had families and had given up their jobs to enlist and fight for the Empire. He requested that the Minister issue a general order that medically fit Black men not be discriminated against by military recruiting officers in Canada.[10]

On November 25, 1915, Lieutenant-Colonel George W. Fowler, the officer commanding the 104th Battalion, wrote to the Acting Adjutant-General, 6th Division, Halifax, N.S., requesting approval to discharge the twenty Black soldiers, primarily on the basis of race. "I have been fortunate to have secured a very fine class of recruits," he wrote, "and I did not think it fair to these men that they should have to mingle with Negroes."[11]

On the same date, Hughes replied to Richards' letter, indicating that he had issued instructions permitting Black men to enlist in any battalion. He also pledged to have his adjutant-general report immediately on the situation at Camp Sussex.[12]

Acting Adjutant-General Hodgins, on November 29, wrote to the General Officer, 6th Division, Halifax. He requested a full report on the refusal of the 104th Battalion to accept the twenty enlisted soldiers. The letter confirmed Hughes' position. "A great many complaints have been received from the coloured men in regard to their treatment," Hodgins wrote, "and the Honourable Minister has given instructions that the coloured men are to be permitted to enlist in any battalion."[13]

The directives from the Minister were straightforward and explicit. The continuing rejection experienced by Blacks, however, suggests that his orders were not taken seriously in many parts of the country. Robin Winks perceptively described the reality of the situation: "Having often ignored the orders of his superiors, Hughes discovered that amidst the confusion of war his subordinates could find ways of ignoring him. Very few Negroes were accepted for military service."[14]

Meanwhile, in Ontario, Black leaders were still searching for a way for Black men to serve their beloved country. They were not about to accept rejection as the final, conclusive word. As far as they were concerned, the issue was still very much open for debate. In a few instances, influential citizens provided tangible support for the war effort by raising units for overseas service at their own expense. This was, of course, subject to the approval of the Department of Militia and Defence.

As a further concrete indication of the intense desire of Blacks to participate in the War, the publisher of a Black newspaper in Toronto offered to raise a platoon of soldiers. Despite the fact that his patriotic proposal received official authorization, the implementation of his scheme became an exercise in frustration and embarrassment. Wrote Barbara Wilson:

[When] J. R. B. Whitney, publisher of the Canadian Observer, *of-*

fered to raise a unit of 150 Coloured soldiers in November 1915, he was told by Sir Sam Hughes that these people can form a platoon in any battalion now. There is nothing in the world to stop them.

Hughes failed to mention that the platoon would have to be accepted by the commanding officer of an authorized battalion before it could be formed. On the strength of Hughes' letter, Whitney began his recruiting campaign in the pages of the Canadian Observer.

When Whitney asked in January 1916 for a Coloured chap in the 80th Battalion to accompany him on a recruiting trip to London, Chatham and Windsor, officers at headquarters realized for the first time that the proposed unit was not attached to any unit.

After General Logie reported in March that no commanding officer was willing to accept the platoon, he was instructed to tell Whitney that permission to recruit cannot be granted.[15]

The outright, overt rejection of the Black platoon placed Whitney in a rather awkward position, to say the least. He was at a loss as to what to tell the men who had expressed their willingness to enlist. Many of the volunteers recruited by Whitney had already committed themselves to joining the Army. Some had quit their jobs, and others had made alternative living arrangements for their wives and families.

Whitney refused to accept the tardy negative response, and he asked that his plan to recruit a Black platoon be reconsidered. In a letter to Hughes on April 18, 1916, he reminded Hughes of his earlier assertion that "these people can form a platoon in any battalion now. There is nothing in the world to stop them."[16] Whitney further vented his frustration by appealing to the Minister for redress:

Through the columns of the Canadian Observer *(the official organ of the Coloured Race in Canada), I have published a call for recruits for the Coloured Platoon. Many have responded to the call, and are eagerly waiting to be uniformed in the King's colours. The Race as a whole is looking forward to the outcome of the Coloured Platoon. I trust that you will see to it that the Coloured Platoon will be placed with some battalion, otherwise there will be a great disappointment with the Race.*[17]

Whitney's appeal to the top military official in the country was unsuccessful, and it soon became apparent that the commanding and recruiting officers were actually deciding the policy concerning Black enlistment. By this time, the War had been under way for almost two years. A blood-bath was taking place on the battlefields of France and Belgium. Canadian troops had had their baptism of fire in early 1915, and by 1916, casualties were reaching alarming proportions.

The lack of sufficient reinforcements for battalions at the front was becoming a serious national problem. Throughout the country, that divisive word conscription was being heard more and more. And still the issue of accepting or continuing the unofficial policy of rejecting Black volunteers had not been resolved by the civilian and military hierarchy.

Prior to the rejection of Whitney's plan, the issue reached the floor of the House of Commons, the highest decision-making body in the land. William Pugsley, Member for Saint John and a former premier of New Brunswick, asked if any effective steps had been taken towards Black enlistment or the formation of a Black regiment. Pugsley reported that representations had been made by Black citizens of New Brunswick and Ontario and that he had brought the matter to the attention of the House on at least two previous occasions. It was his understanding that the Minister of Militia and Defence was considering raising a Black battalion. Pugsley described the Black community's mood of dissatisfaction:

There is a good deal of complaint and a very considerable amount of feeling among our coloured citizens that they have not been treated fairly. They have been told that their services would be accepted, and when they have gone to the recruiting office where they were told to go, they have been sent away without receiving any satisfaction.[18]

The Acting Minister of Militia and Defence, A. Edward Kemp, responded:

I understand there are a number of coloured people in the various units throughout the country; but I am not aware that any effort has so far been made to organize a unit composed wholly of coloured citizens. Some steps may have been taken, but I have no information to that effect at present. I shall make inquiries.[19]

From the other side of the country, Colonel Ogilvie, the officer commanding Military District 11, Victoria, B.C., expressed some rigid views on the matter. In a letter to Militia Council headquarters, dated December 9, 1915, he said that the colour line in British Columbia was sharply drawn compared with eastern Canada. Ogilvie's recommendations left no room for misinterpretation:

Several cases of coloured applicants for enlistment have been reported on by Officers Commanding units and the universal opinion is that if this were allowed it would do much harm, as white men here will not serve in the same ranks with negros [sic] or coloured persons.[20]

He recommended that authority be granted to enlist Black men in a separate unit and that they be sent forward as a draft to join similar units organized in the East.[21]

A rather ambiguous memorandum from Major-General Gwatkin to the adjutant-generals on December 22, 1915, clouded the issue. Gwatkin appeared to favour retention of the existing recruiting methods, which admitted a few token Blacks into the various units at the discretion of commanding officers. He wrote:

The fiat has gone forth: There is to be no coloured line, coloured battalions are not to be raised; coloured men are to be allowed to enlist in any battalion of the C.E.F.

But commanding officers (or some of them) object, and what is to be done?

It would be humiliating to the coloured men themselves to serve in a battalion where they were not wanted, and I think that your own is the best solution of the difficulty. [22]

Word came on March 11, 1916, from Brigadier-General E. A. Cruikshank, the officer commanding Military District 13, Alberta, favouring the formation of a segregated Black overseas battalion. He summarized the situation in that province:

In my opinion it would not be advisable to enlist Negroes or other coloured men in a white battalion, and from information in my possession it would appear to me to be practicable to raise an entire battalion in this province, providing the men enlist in the numbers anticipated. [23]

Finally, in April 1916, after almost two years of contradictions and indecision, Gwatkin issued a memorandum that outlined several courses of action. As a preamble, he put forth some extremely disparaging opinions and negative presumptions concerning the loyalty and combat capabilities of Black men. Among other things, he wrote, "In France, in the firing line, there is no place for a black battalion, C.E.F. It would be eyed askance; it would crowd out a white battalion; and it would be difficult to re-inforce [sic]." [24]

Gwatkin recommended that the present system of permitting individual Blacks to enlist in white battalions at the discretion of commanding officers be continued. He further suggested they be allowed to form one or more labour battalions.

It would appear that Gwatkin and many other military officials of the day were either unaware of, or prepared to ignore, the fact that Black combat troops had performed admirably in previous wars. Nevertheless, Gwatkin's memo became the basis for the recruitment of a segregated Black construction battalion. On May 11, 1916, the British War Office in London cabled the Governor-General expressing its willingness to accept such a unit. [25]

NO. 2 CONSTRUCTION BATTALION, CEF

The No. 2 Construction Battalion, CEF, the first and only Black battalion in Canadian military history, was authorized on July 5, 1916, with headquarters at Pictou, N.S. The unit was under the command of Lieutenant-Colonel Daniel Hugh Sutherland, a railroad contractor from River John, N.S.

Other officers were Captain David Anderson, Springhill, N.S.; Captain John Sidney Davie, Liverpool, England; Captain Arthur John Gayfer, Edmonton, Alta.; Captain James Stuart Grant, Ottawa, Ont.; Captain Roderick Livingston, Dartmouth, N.S.; Captain Kenneth Allan Morrison, Ottawa; Captain Dan Murray (MO), Tatamagouche, N.S.; the Reverend Captain William A. White (Chaplain), Truro, N.S.; Captain William Lee Young, Calgary, Alta.; Lieutenant Isaac Logan Barnhill, Truro; Lieutenant Ernest N. Halton Fyles, Ottawa; Lieutenant James Bertram Hayes, Halifax, N.S.; Lieutenant Samuel Clifford Hood, Yarmouth, N.S.; Lieutenant Gillan Christie Machean, Ottawa; Lieutenant Herbert Boyne MacLean, Pictou; Lieutenant Russell Roderick R. MacLean, Moncton, N.B.; Lieutenant George Henry Parker, Truro; and Lieutenant Leslie Bruce Young, Hamilton, Ont.

The Chaplain of the Battalion, the Reverend Captain William A. White, was a Black Baptist minister from Truro. This native of Williamsburg, Va., was reported to be the only Black commissioned officer in the British Forces during World War I.[1] By contrast, six hundred Black Americans were commissioned as officers in the United States Armed Forces during the War.[2]

The unique status of the Battalion can be measured by the fact that Lieutenant-Colonel Sutherland was authorized to deal directly with the Militia Council in Ottawa and by-pass the normal channels of command in Halifax.[3] The Battalion was also granted special authority to recruit in all provinces, wherever Black people were residing. Due to the widespread rejection of Black volunteers, it was nationally recognized that the Battalion would not compete with other units.

No. 2 Construction Battalion, CEF, Truro, N.S.

Despite previous rejections and the segregated status of the Battalion, Black men and boys throughout the country immediately volunteered for duty. Nova Scotia provided the largest number of recruits (approximately three hundred). It was estimated that about two hundred Black men were employed in the coal mines of Nova Scotia and therefore were not eligible for enlistment.

Early recruits from the Halifax-Dartmouth area included John Lambert, William Tolliver, James Parris, Samuel Collins and Gilbert Richard Lattimore. Lattimore (931001), who joined the unit on July 19, 1916, was apparently the first to sign up. In Upper Hammonds Plains, N.S., seventeen-year-old Gordon Charles Wilson hitched up his father's horse and wagon and travelled twenty miles to Halifax, where he was examined medically and inducted into the Battalion. Arthur and William Ware of Calgary journeyed from the family homestead and proudly donned Canadian uniforms; they were sons of the legendary Black cowboy John Ware. At least eleven of the twenty New Brunswick soldiers who had been turned away from Camp Sussex became members of the Battalion. But there is no available record of the fate of the other nine.

The proposed make-up of the Battalion, consisting of 1,049 men of all ranks, including attached, was three headquarters officers, 280 other ranks, one headquarters (attached) officer and four companies (A,B,C,D), each consisting of one captain and two lieutenants.

The unit was stationed at Pictou for approximately three months. The Bob Brown building, located on the Market Wharf, Water Street, served as barracks for the troops. The building had been previously occupied by members of the 106th Battalion, CEF.

Reports indicate that the building was demolished more than

The Reverend Captain William A. White, Chaplain, No. 2 Construction Battalion, is reported to have been the only Black commissioned officer in the British Forces during World War I.

World War I veterans William Carter (left) and Gordon Charles Wilson proudly display a photo of their old company, A, No. 2 Construction Battalion.

twenty-five years ago. The Market Wharf, or what remains of it, is now a picture of decay and disrepair, with no lingering signs of military history. A tourist visiting the area would never know that Canada's only Black battalion assembled there some seventy years before.

Two former residents of Pictou, Patricia McGuire and her brother Russell Hayden, will always remember the Market Wharf. They also have fond memories of the Black soldiers stationed there in 1916. Hayden, then a ten-year-old boy, fell into Pictou Harbour and was rescued by one of the soldiers. McGuire, who was eight years old at the time, vividly recalled the incident:

We were playing on the Market Wharf, Russell and I and several friends. Russell had been born with cerebral palsy, and at ten he was just learning to walk. He lost his balance and tumbled into the water. One of the soldiers came running and jumped into the water fully clothed. He reached Russell just in time and carried him home to our mother. She was so grateful that she supplied the soldiers with home-baking until they left Pictou. Russell is now seventy-eight and still going strong.[4]

George McCullion, an eighty-seven-year-old resident of Pictou,

Halifax members of the No. 2 Construction Battalion. Private James Parris (left) enlisted on July 19, 1916, and Private Vincent Carvery enlisted on January 8, 1917. Both are deceased.

The Ware brothers, Private Arthur N. (left) and Private William J., Alberta, sons of the legendary Black cowboy John Ware, enlisted in the No. 2 Construction Battalion in November 1916.

recalled playing baseball and socializing with members of the Battalion:

We had a local ball team, and we would challenge the soldiers to a game on a regular basis. When we were not playing ball, we would sit around the wharf singing and harmonizing. Some of the soldiers were quite young. We had a lot of fun and got along swell.[5]

On August 19, 1916, Lieutenant-Colonel Sutherland reported that there were 180 recruits at Pictou. He expected to recruit five hundred in the Maritimes, one company in Ontario and another in western Canada. He also proposed to move the headquarters from Pictou to Truro, where he felt the presence of a Black community would stimulate recruiting.[6] Pictou had no Black residents in 1916, and seventy years later, there are still few, if any, in that town.

On September 9, 1916, battalion headquarters were relocated to Truro, leaving one hundred men in Pictou to take on recruits. (Shortly after arriving in Truro, the Black soldiers were subjected to segregated seating in the balcony of the local theatre. Various protests and the intervention of battalion officers led to the elimination of that discriminatory policy.)

Recruitment for the unit, however, continued to be a problem. Late in 1916 and during the early months of 1917, approximately 165 Black Americans were recruited. It seems that Canadian and American authorities entered into some sort of arrangement to facilitate the enlistment of Black Americans into the Canadian Army, even though the United States did not enter the War until April 1917. In any event, a senior Canadian immigration official expressed concern about allowing a large number of Black men to gain a foothold in Canada.[7]

In November 1916, to encourage enlistment, the Battalion Band, under the direction of Bandmaster Sergeant William J. Thomas, performed at a recruiting concert in the First Presbyterian Church Hall in New Glasgow, N.S. As well, the Chaplain, Rev. Capt. White, gave a stirring speech. Following the entertainment and speeches, a number of committees were organized to enhance enlistment. After the concert in New Glasgow, the Band and several officers made a short recruiting trip throughout the province, and fifty men were secured in one week. Several months after authorization, however, the Battalion was still understrength.

Also in November 1916, Sutherland requested permission to recruit in the British West Indies. He said there would be no difficulty in building a company of 250 men in a few weeks.[8] But there is no record indicating that permission was granted.

The difficulty the military authorities encountered in recruiting approximately one thousand Black volunteers may be attributed to a number of factors: the previous rejection and humiliation of Black volunteers; the Black objection to serving in a segregated non-combatant labour battalion; and the blatant exclusion of Black immigrants, particularly in western Canada.

Only twenty men from the four western provinces enlisted in the Battalion, even though Sutherland had optimistically assumed a whole company could be recruited. In *The Promised Land*, author Pierre Berton provided some candid statistical data on the impact of immigration restrictions on Blacks. "In its efforts to keep the West racially pure," he wrote, "the Department of Immigration was hugely successful. In 1901 there were ninety-eight Blacks on the prairies. In 1911, after the greatest immigration boom in the nation's history, there were only 1,524."[9]

In December 1916, Sutherland received word from Ottawa that the Battalion was needed overseas as soon as possible. He replied that the unit would be ready for overseas service by the last week

New Brunswick members of the No. 2 Construction Battalion Band. Front row (left to right): Herbert Nichols, George Richard Dixon, Bandmaster Sergeant George William Stewart, A. Seymour Tyler and Harold Bushfan. Back row (left to right): Albert Carty, Fred Charles Dixon, Percy William Thomas and James Albert Sadlier.

of February 1917 and that, although the Battalion was still recruiting, it had reached a strength of 575.[10]

While in training, the unit received an urgent call for steel rails in France. Two hundred and fifty men were dispatched to New Brunswick to pick up rails along the Grand Trunk sidings. In Edmundston, N.B., an outbreak of pneumonia occurred among the soldiers. Nurses and drugs were sent from Halifax to combat the problem. One soldier, Private John R. Lambert of Halifax, died in hospital from the illness.[11]

All the companies then converged on Truro, and they were mobilized as a battalion on March 17, 1917. Canada's Black battalion had now come together, literally from across the North American continent. The little railroad town of Truro, the hub of Nova Scotia, was but a brief stop on the long, stressful road to France. The men eagerly awaited their sailing orders, as well as the unknown adventures and perils that lay ahead.

Prior to embarking for overseas duty, the Battalion, led by its own brass band, held a street parade in Dartmouth. Almost seventy years later, that parade still awakened some long-cherished memories and emotions. Edith Colley, a lifelong resident of that city, recalled:

It was a lovely spring day when the Battalion came marching down

Ochterloney Street. I was only a young girl, but I can still remember that day. The Band was playing the "Colonel Bogey March." The soldiers all looked so smart. Their buttons and boots were shining, and they were marching proudly and so straight. It was just a picture to behold; it was splendid. A day or two later, they all sailed away for France. I'll never forget that parade as long as I live.[12]

Mabel Saunders, a resident of East Preston, N.S., was living in Dartmouth in 1917. She emotionally remembered the day the Battalion paraded through town:

I saw that parade on Prince Albert Road. I was standing by my gate when they came marching by with their chests stuck out and the Band playing. I can't tell you exactly how many, but there was a large crowd of soldiers marching up the street. Everybody was out watching: Black people and white people, waving their hands, cheering and clapping. I can imagine that I can see them now, were they marching. They were proudly marching off to war. It was a nice sight to see, but a sad one. A lot of people felt sad to know that the boys were going overseas. Some were only sixteen or seventeen and had put their ages up to get in the Army. I remember one local boy, Louis Middleton. He was underage, but he got into No. 2 by putting up his age.[13]

Saunders remembered the controversy over the rejection of Black volunteers prior to the establishment of the Battalion. She still had some strong opinions on that issue:

Some of the men were very bitter and disappointed because they were not being accepted into the Army. They wanted to go and could not see why they were not able to go. They were men the same as everybody else. There was considerable joy and happiness among Black people when No. 2 was formed. The men especially felt good about it because they really wanted to go away, to see what the War was all about.[14]

The Battalion, at a strength of nineteen officers and 605 men of other ranks, embarked from Pier 2 in Halifax on March 28, 1917. After a ten-day voyage through submarine-infested waters aboard the SS *Southland*, the unit arrived in Liverpool, England.

In early May 1917, due to being understrength, orders were received to change the status of the Battalion to a company. The unit proceeded to France and the Swiss border, where it was attached to the Canadian Forestry Corps, CEF. The majority of the men served at Lajoux in the Jura Mountains, while smaller detachments joined Forestry units at Péronne and Alençon.

The unit was commended for its discipline and faithful service while attached to the Forestry Corps. Some of the men were eventually assigned to line units and participated in trench combat. In early 1919, following the Armistice of November 11, 1918, the unit returned to Canada, where it was officially disbanded on September 15, 1920. The No. 2 Construction Battalion thus faded away into the dusty annals of Canadian military history.

106TH BATTALION, CEF

It is a rather incredible fact of Canadian history that, during the early years of World War I, Black volunteers were not altogether welcome in the Armed Forces. As indicated in the introduction, however, Black volunteers did serve in a number of combat units; not all of them served in the No. 2 Construction Battalion, CEF.

One of the units that enlisted a number of Blacks was the 106th Battalion, Nova Scotia Rifles, CEF, which was authorized on November 8, 1915. Its headquarters were located in Truro, where three of its companies were stationed; the fourth company was stationed in Springhill. Recruits were drawn from various parts of the province, as well as from Prince Edward Island, New Brunswick and Newfoundland.

Shortly after the Battalion began recruiting, the controversy over Black volunteers once again reared its ugly head. The issue of accepting or rejecting Blacks became the concern and responsibility of the Commanding Officer, Lieutenant-Colonel W. H. Allen.

The matter came to the fore as a result of the efforts of one Samuel Reese to enlist in the Army. Reese, a Black native of British Guiana residing in Truro, tried to join the Composite Battalion, CEF, and the Royal Canadian Regiment, CEF.[1] The Adjutant, Captain M. E. Roscoe, refused to accept Reese unless he could recruit a certain number of his fellow Black countrymen. At the same time, Reese was referred to Allen for enlistment in the 106th Battalion. Reese pursued the matter further by seeking the assistance of the Reverend William A. White, then the Pastor of the Zion Baptist Church in Truro. White, in turn, appealed directly to Allen.[2]

In an effort to keep headquarters apprised of the situation and to elicit support for his decision, Allen wrote to Halifax on December 14, 1915, outlining the method he was using to resolve the problem:

After a recruiting meeting in Truro several weeks ago, a coloured

Sydney Morgan Jones, Halifax, N.S., points to Pier 2, where, as Private Jones, 106th Battalion, he embarked for overseas service on July 15, 1919, aboard the SS *Empress of Britain*. He was a member of the Reunion Advisory Committee.

minister, Rev. Mr. White, approached me in regard to the matter, and I told him if he would get in touch with the coloured men throughout Nova Scotia, and raise enough for a platoon, I would take this platoon into my Regiment. He promised to get busy, but to date, I have only received about six names. Since that time, word has come from Ottawa that there is to be no distinction of colour for enlistments.[3]

Allen pointed out that, after it became known that "the colour bar" had been removed, several white men who had been about to sign up refused to do so. He felt that Blacks should do their share in defending the Empire, and he believed that some of them would make good soldiers. Allen did, however, express a strong preference for white soldiers. He suggested that the best approach would be to keep Black and white men separated. "I trust that some solution may be found by which the services of coloured men may be utilized," he wrote. "In the meantime, I am not encouraging the enlistment of coloured men in the 106th Battalion. . . ."[4]

In any event, approximately sixteen Black volunteers were accepted into the Battalion from December 1915 to July 1916.

Private James A. Clyke, Truro, N.S., 106th Battalion, enlisted on June 3, 1916, and served in England and France.

Jeremiah (Jerry) Jones, 106th Battalion, enlisted in Truro, N.S., on June 19, 1916. On arrival overseas, he was assigned to the Royal Canadian Regiment in France. He was recommended for the Distinguished Conduct Medal.

Gunner Robert James Bowen, Halifax, N.S., enlisted in the Royal Canadian Artillery on October 6, 1917. From October 28, 1919, until April 20, 1920, he served as a special guard with the Canadian Military Police Corps.

(Samuel Reese, meanwhile, became a corporal in the No. 2 Construction Battalion.) In May 1916, Lieutenant-Colonel Robert Innis was appointed Commanding Officer. Indeed, it may be no coincidence that the majority of Black volunteers were accepted into the unit after his appointment.

The Black soldiers were not segregated into a specific platoon, but were dispersed throughout the Battalion's four companies. There is no question that the intervention of White and the verbal agreement between he and Allen to accept a Black platoon were major factors in opening the door to Black enlistment in that particular unit.

Eighty-six-year-old Sydney Morgan Jones of Halifax, a native of Truro, was one of the Black volunteers in the Battalion. He recalled the excitement of being accepted. "The realization that sixteen Blacks were in the Battalion was an exciting development," he said. "The fact that I, a fifteen-year-old boy, was one of them gave me an intense feeling of pride."[5]

On July 15, 1916, the Battalion left for England aboard the SS *Empress of Britain*. The 106th did not see action as a unit, but instead was broken up to provide reinforcements for front-line battalions that were understrength after suffering heavy casualties on the battlefields of France.

One of the Black volunteers, Jeremiah (Jerry) Jones, also from Truro, joined the Royal Canadian Regiment in the trenches. He gained a measure of fame by clearing out a German dug-out and capturing the survivors and their machine gun. Although people say he was recommended for a Distinguished Conduct Medal, there is no documentation to suggest he received any such decoration.

Rollie and Norman Ash, teenaged brothers from Antigonish, N.S., joined the 106th and, later, the 85th Battalion, CEF. They made the supreme sacrifice while serving King and Country. The late Frank Ash, a World War II veteran formerly of Halifax, told how his brothers ran away from home to enlist in the Armed Forces:

Rollie and Norman were overseas for about a year when my mother received word that they were missing in action. They were fighting in France, at the time with the 85th Battalion. Later on, my mother received two Silver Crosses, indicating that they were considered dead.[6]

Some Black volunteers also served in other CEF combat units, including the 25th Battalion, the 88th Battalion, the Nova Scotia Regiment, the 1st Depot Battalion, the 102nd Battalion, the 1st Quebec Regiment and the 116th Battalion.

CONSCRIPTION

By 1917, thousands of Canadian soldiers had been killed or wounded on the battlefields of France. By the cessation of hostilities in 1918, Canadian casualties were approximately sixty thousand dead or missing and 173,000 wounded.

To reinforce the depleted troops, Ottawa passed the Military Service Act on August 29, 1917. The Act, with some exceptions, made every British subject between the ages of twenty and forty-five who was, or had been, since August 4, 1914, residing in Canada liable for active service. Conscription had become the law of the land.

The Act was an ironic twist for Black patriots who had tried to serve their country and who had been rejected by a military establishment that could not accept the concept of Black Canadians in arms. Men who from 1914 to 1916 had been prohibited from enlisting in the Armed Forces were now subject to conscription.

As a result, some embittered Blacks refused to respond to the call-up notices. This led to Blacks being stopped on the streets and asked to show exception documents. Those without such papers were forcibly inducted into the Army. Hilda Lambert of Halifax, N.S., recalled an incident involving her father:

My father, who was in his late forties, was coming home from work when the military police approached him. They took him to the Armouries to be conscripted into the Army. He told them he had two sons fighting overseas, while they stayed at home sitting on their butts. After about two hours, they decided to release him.[1]

John Crawley, an eighty-five-year-old resident of North Preston, N.S., remembered his brush with conscription officials:

I was around eighteen years of age, and I had gone to Dartmouth with my horse and wagon to pick up some groceries. The conscription officers grabbed me for the Army. My brother-in-law Harry Sparks told them that I was too young. They took both of us to Halifax. My father came in, and they let me go. Harry Sparks was conscripted into the Army and ended up overseas.[2]

Private William (Harry) Sparks (seated), Lake Loon, Halifax County, N.S., died on July 3, 1972. Soldiers standing are unidentified.

Veteran Isaac Phills of Dartmouth, N.S., recalled the irony created by conscription:

In Sydney after the War started, quite a few Blacks volunteered for active service and were told point blank, "We don't want you. This is a white man's war." However, around 1917 the Canadian Army was up against it; they had lost a lot of men in France. At that point, they were willing to take anyone. Conscription came in, and then they took Blacks and whites. You had no choice—you had to go.[3]

The conscription of Blacks into the Army, however, also created dilemmas for military authorities who wanted to maintain the status quo of racial segregation. Phills, one of approximately sixty conscripted Blacks in one unit, recalled that, after receiving training alongside white conscripts in Canada, on arrival in England Black soldiers were placed in a segregated unit and assigned to fatigue and labour duties.[4] At the time, there was some indication that Black conscripts, although trained as infantry, would be stationed with the segregated No. 2 Construction Battalion, CEF. That did not materialize, however, probably because of the acute shortage of combat troops.

Eventually, the Black conscripts were designated as reinforcements for the 85th Battalion, CEF. But before they could join that unit, the Armistice was signed, and hostilities came to an end. Nonetheless, at the end of the War, the Black soldiers, both volunteers and conscripts, could sing with true meaning the words of that old Negro spiritual "Down By the Riverside":

Going to lay down my sword and shield
Down by the riverside
And study war no more.

CHAPTER
Nọ 5

THE SEARCH
FOR VETERANS

On May 19, 1977, the Nova Scotia legislature enacted the incorporation of The Society for the Protection and Preservation of Black Culture in Nova Scotia (also known as the Black Cultural Society), whose first annual meeting was held in Halifax the following August. Before the Society was even incorporated, however, a steering committee had developed goals concerning a Black cultural centre. One of the recommendations said that "the achievements and activities of Black people in Nova Scotia be recognized."

Four years later, the Society set out to fulfil that goal. In 1981, it approved a motion to sponsor its first public event, a reunion-and-recognition weekend for veterans of World War I. Subsequently, a planning committee was formed to work on the events, tentatively scheduled for the fall of 1982. One of the initial tasks, therefore, was to locate and contact surviving veterans.

The Committee quickly discovered that at least five veterans were residing in the Halifax-Dartmouth area: Sydney Morgan Jones, Gordon Charles Wilson, Albert David Deleon, Isaac Phills and John R. Pannill. A copy of the nominal roll of the No. 2 Construction Battalion, CEF, was then obtained, and it confirmed that the largest group of veterans was in Nova Scotia. The nominal roll was broken down by counties, and the names were forwarded to society members. A province-wide search revealed that only a small number of World War I veterans was still living.

It was discovered that in the Annapolis and Digby areas surviving veterans included James Elmer Cromwell, William F. Guy, Wallace Pleasant (residing in Sunnybrook Hospital, Toronto, Ont.) and Malcolm Jarvis (residing in Cambridge, Mass.). Information from Montreal, Que., indicated that John W. Hamilton and George W. Harrison were living there, as was Alfred West. In Halifax, a local historian said William Carter was a Great War veteran.

Contact with A. Seymour Tyler of Lakeville Corner, N.B., a

Members of the Reunion Advisory Committee finalize plans for the reunion-and-recognition events. Left to right: veteran Isaac Phills, Reunion Co-chairperson Calvin Ruck, veteran Gordon Charles Wilson and veteran Sydney Morgan Jones.

James Elmer Cromwell (left), Southville, Digby County, N.S., and John Smith, Middleton, N.S., were buddies in the No. 2 Construction Battalion. On September 7, 1984, they met for the first time since returning home in 1919. Each was unaware that the other was still alive.

Albert David Deleon, Halifax, N.S., joined the Army on November 11, 1917, and served with the Canadian Forestry Corps in the United Kingdom and France. Deleon is participating in a wheelchair race at a veteran's sports day. He is flanked by Camp Hill employees Kay Youle (left) and Meg Pryde. He passed away in 1986.

veteran of both World Wars, led to the whereabouts of Jack Claybourne. Also in New Brunswick, Saint John's Clifford Skinner, a member of the Reunion Planning Committee, provided the names of Percy Richards, Earl Leek and Percy Howe. A trip to Middleton, N.S., turned up John Smith, who served with the No. 2 Construction Battalion and, in World War II, the Veteran's Guard. Finally, veteran Gordon Charles Wilson informed the Committee that Robert Shepard was living in New Glasgow, N.S., and A. Benjamin Elms in Monastery, N.S.

Some of the methods used to reach surviving veterans did not produce positive results. Letters to people in Ontario and Boston, Mass., did not elicit any response, nor did an ad in the Royal Canadian Legion magazine, *The Legionnaire*.

The Reunion Planning Committee also tried to get funding for the weekend's activities. Favourable responses were received from veteran's organizations, private businesses, community groups, church organizations and provincial and federal government agencies.

Members of the Reunion Advisory Committee, which included Sydney Morgan Jones, Isaac Phills and Gordon Charles Wilson, heartily approved the proposed events: a reunion banquet, reception, bus tour and church service. With the news that nine veterans planned to attend the reunion-and-recognition ceremonies, the stage was set for an exciting and historic weekend.

REUNION
AND RECOGNITION

The highlight of the weekend was the Reunion and Recognition Banquet, held on Friday, November 12. The next day, commenting on the significance of the event, the Halifax *Mail-Star* reported, "The Imperial Ballroom at the Lord Nelson Hotel was packed last night with nearly 300 guests for the first and perhaps only reunion of Black First World War Veterans."[1]

It was truly a night to remember.

The evening got under way with the ageing veterans marching smartly into the ballroom to the nostalgic strains of a favourite World War I song, "It's a Long Way to Tipperary." The procession was enthusiastically greeted by an overwhelming standing ovation. Following initial formalities—the invocation grace delivered by the Reverend W. P. Oliver and the introduction of the veterans and other head-table guests by Master of Ceremonies Wayne Adams—the President of The Society for the Protection and Preservation of Black Culture in Nova Scotia (also known as the Black Cultural Society), H. A. J. Wedderburn, extended a cordial welcome to the veterans. In a brief speech, he explained the motivation behind the event:

A famous Nova Scotian once said that for a people to be great they must gather onto themselves the memorabilia of their past achievements and must honour their ancestors who have accomplished, and those things must be preserved for future generations. The Cultural Society tonight is trying to do just that. We are honouring the men who fought to make Canada great, and we are also here to remember those men who died to make the country great.

Wedderburn then called for a hearty round of applause for the veterans, which drew another thunderous ovation. He also thanked members of the Stadacona Band for their appropriate music from the Great War era. Captain George Borden, a member of the Reunion Planning Committee, presented the toast to the Queen.

A number of representatives of the Federal Government, vet-

The nine World War I veterans who attended the Reunion and Recognition Banquet, November 12, 1982. Front row (left to right): William Carter, Halifax; John W. Hamilton, Montreal; Percy J. Richards, Saint John; Gordon Charles Wilson, Halifax; Albert David Deleon, Halifax. Back row (left to right): A. Seymour Tyler, Lakeville Corner; Sydney Morgan Jones, Halifax; Isaac Phills, Dartmouth; John R. Pannill, Halifax.

eran's organizations, church groups and community organizations extended greetings and good wishes to the veterans. They included J. Albert Walker, First Vice-President, Dominion Command, Army, Navy and Air Force Veterans of Canada; Leo Gargan, President, Nova Scotia Command, Army, Navy and Air Force Veterans of Canada; Churchill Smith, Moderator, African United Baptist Association of Nova Scotia; George F. McCurdy, Director, Nova Scotia Human Rights Commission; Raymond Richards, President, Pride of Race, Unity, Dignity, Education (PRUDE), Saint John, N.B.; and Clifford Skinner, Reunion Planning Committee, also Saint John.

Greetings
Raymond Richards, President,
Pride of Race, Unity, Dignity, Education (PRUDE),
Saint John, N.B.

Good evening ladies and gentlemen. It is my pleasure to bring greetings on behalf of our organization to the surviving veterans of the No. 2 Construction Battalion and other World War I units who are present on this most memorable occasion.

Without a doubt, it is a real honour to stand before you veterans as a tangible indication that you have not been forgotten and that your hardships and sacrifices were not in vain.

It is definitely time that you were honoured and recognized in this fitting manner, so that members of the Black community and Canadians in general can be made much more aware and proud of your service to King and Country under very difficult circumstances. You deserve a place of honour and respect in the military history of this great country, side by side with your white comrades.

As I speak to you tonight with pride and appreciation, I am mindful of the fact that you were the instruments, the men, through which our freedom was made possible.

We should never let people forget these men and all the other Black military men who served this country to preserve freedom for all. I would like to congratulate the officers and members of the Black Cultural Society for a fine effort here tonight.

Thank you Mr. Chairman.

Greetings
Clifford Skinner,
Reunion Planning Committee,
Saint John, N.B.

Mr. Chairman, this is one of the most heart-warming occasions that I have ever had the pleasure to attend. I was appointed as a representative in New Brunswick to help out with this reunion, and you would be surprised at the warmth and feeling that comes from New Brunswick.

I just want to say it is a real pleasure to be here tonight, and my heart is here in Nova Scotia.

Thank you.

Greetings
Churchill S. Smith, Moderator,
African United Baptist Association of Nova Scotia

Mr. Chairman, honourable clergy, distinguished head-table guests, I feel very honoured to be here tonight, on this very special occasion, as we honour and pay tribute to our World War I veterans at this reunion dinner.

I want to take this opportunity to bring greetings to you on behalf of the African United Baptist Association of Nova Scotia.

We recognize the great contribution you have made in the defence of our country during the war years. We ask God's richest blessings and good health to all of you in the years ahead.

Greetings
*J. Albert Walker, First Vice-President,
Dominion Command, Army, Navy and Air Force
Veterans of Canada*

On behalf of the Dominion Command of the Army, Navy and Air Force Veterans of Canada and our president, Mr. Ron Dunn, who is unable to be here, I have been given the honour to bring you greetings.

I might say that it was our honour on Monday of this week to make two of the veterans who are at the head table honorary members of our organization, Comrade Charles Wilson and Comrade Sydney Jones.

And I might also say, on behalf of the army, navy and air force veterans in Nova Scotia, that we are prepared to make every First World War veteran an honorary member of our organization. I would only ask that those who know where they are to communicate with me or with the Provincial Command Secretary so we can make contact with them.

On behalf of the Army, Navy and Air Force Veterans of Canada, I want to thank you, Mr. Chairman, and you, Mr. Ruck, for the work you have done.

Thank you again.

Greetings
*Leo Gargan, President,
Nova Scotia Command, Army, Navy and Air Force
Veterans of Canada*

I consider it a great pleasure and a singular honour to bring greetings and salutations on such a momentous occasion as this evening.

I say on behalf of all the Nova Scotian veterans of the Army, Navy and Air Force in Canada to come here and break bread this evening is indeed a great and sincere pleasure.

And to our World War I veterans, I salute you on behalf of all our units in Nova Scotia.

Thank you.

Greetings
*George F. McCurdy, Director,
Nova Scotia Human Rights Commission*

Mr. Chairman, on behalf of the Nova Scotia Human Rights Commission, I am pleased to join with the countless friends of the veterans and survivors of the No. 2 Construction Battalion and other World War I units and this distinguished gathering in paying fitting and worthwhile tribute to these gallant men.

It is important, Mr. Chairman, to put Black history in its proper perspective. We must from time to time remind our fellow citizens that Blacks have helped to build this nation, that we have fought its wars, we have dreamed its dreams, have contributed to its greatness and also felt the weight of its failures.

You, the survivors and veterans of World War I, in my judgement, epitomize the real profiles and courage of Black history. You served, gentlemen, for the ideals of freedom, justice, equality and peace, in spite of the limited acceptance of Black Canadians at that particular time. You have paid your dues and I salute you. We salute you.

Thank you.

After the greetings, W. P. Oliver commemorated departed veterans:

I do not know the exact number who paid the supreme sacrifice and who are numbered with the thousands of their comrades who now lie in Flanders Fields. However, I am sure that the remaining group with us tonight, of that gallant and loyal six hundred, will remember them one by one and name by name. The veterans served with distinction; they and their padre, Captain White, represented Canadian Blacks in a commendable manner.

Requesting a minute of silence, Oliver recited the Act of Remembrance: "They shall grow not old, as we who are left grow old. Age shall not weary them, nor the years condemn. At the going down of the sun and in the morning, we shall remember them."

Representing John Buchanan, Premier of Nova Scotia, Edmund Morris, Minister of Social Services, delivered the keynote address. He began his memorable and moving oration with a tribute to William Edward Hall, the Black Nova Scotia hero who was awarded the Victoria Cross, the Empire's highest award for valour. He further elated the audience by announcing the establishment of the William Hall Memorial Collection as a lasting memento of this great night. Morris promised to donate books, from his personal library, to the Collection, to be housed in the Black Cultural Centre in Dartmouth.

With respect to the racism encountered by Blacks in their efforts to voluntarily enlist, Morris pulled no punches:

In the outer room amid the muniments and mementoes of Black service to Canada, to King, to Commonwealth and to Liberty there is, against the far wall, a particular corner given over to William Hall.

William Hall was a simple son of the soil, born in 1827 at Horton's Bluff, Nova Scotia. He served on the HMS Shannon. He was almost single-handedly responsible for the relief of Lucknow, and he held the Empire's highest award: the Victoria Cross. The first Canadian and the first man of colour, as it is inscribed on his sepulcher in front of the Hantsport Baptist Church.

When I come through Hantsport I frequently stop to look at the small cairn that now marks the resting place of William Hall. We should think of William Hall tonight in the company of these his gallant brothers.

What a source of pride it should be to you, and to me as your brother, that William Hall, a simple Black farm boy from Horton's Bluff who sleeps forever in the soil of our beloved province, was the first Black man to win the Empire's highest award.

So my mind tonight, in the few minutes I will be with you, goes out to William Hall.

May I be permitted to say to you that, with the consent of the Board, I have determined, not being a man of private wealth but a man of good intent, that I will provide the initial contribution, and it will be thereafter a private life charity, to establish in the great new cultural centre that is now rising a collection of books to memorialize Black history and the Black contribution to our beloved country.

It will start with a few hundred volumes and I will build upon it, God willing, and my sons will do likewise after I am gone. I will establish the William Hall Memorial Collection as a tribute and as a lasting memento of this great night and of the hospitality and affection the Black brothers and sisters have given me throughout my life.

We have come together to honour Black veterans who served in World War I, some who served in World War II.

Into the stormy Atlantic in late March 1917 members of the No. 2 Construction Battalion, nineteen officers and 605 other ranks, embarked for England and onward to France.

It is a curiosity and an irony, and we should not now dwell upon it, love has taken us beyond those years, but it is a fact, that they were not wanted, even in the white man's war.

Yet the spirit that resided in them, the energy and the courage, defined as grace under pressure, inspired them to serve on behalf of their people, their country, their monarch, believing that those things they had inherited from the past would give way to a brighter day.

So it is a final irony, having volunteered and being told in many cases to wait, if we require you we will let you know, that they were sent overseas in the ten days of the War that saw the heaviest submarine activity in the North Atlantic.

Many of them must have wondered, as they traversed the ocean, whether still another crucifix had been added to their Blackness. In England, and onward to France they went, accompanied by Captain White, whose daughter is with us tonight, and sang so beautifully a short while ago "My Buddy." Captain White is believed to have been the only Black commissioned officer in the British Forces during World War I.

So hear the names of those who survived, men now in their eighties, nine of them with us tonight, others not able to be here. Survivors of the great crusade that went to France.

William Carter, from Halifax, with us tonight, who served in the No. 2 Construction Battalion; Jack Claybourne, Fredericton, N.B., No. 2 Construction Battalion; James Elmer Cromwell, Southville, Digby County, No. 2 Construction Battalion; Albert David Deleon, Halifax, N.S., Canadian Forestry Corps, who is present tonight; A. Benjamin Elms, Monastery, N.S., No. 2 Construction Battalion; William Guy, Kentville, N.S., who served with the Nova Scotia Regiment; John Hamilton, from Montreal, Que., who is with us tonight and who served with the No. 2 Construction Battalion; George Harrison, Montreal, Que., No. 2 Construction Battalion; Percy Howe, Fredericton, N.B., 5th CMRS Infantry; Malcolm Jarvis, No. 2 Construction Battalion, now · residing in Cambridge, Mass; Sydney M. Jones, Halifax, N.S., who is with us tonight, served with the 106th Battalion and the Royal Canadian Regiment, wounded at Passendale on the 30th of October 1917. He serves on the Board of Deacons, Cornwallis Street Baptist Church, and he is the manager of the Age and Opportunity Centre of that church; Earl Leek of Fredericton, N.B., served with the 236 Highlanders; John Pannill of Halifax, my dinner companion tonight, who served in the Merchant Navy; Isaac Phills of Dartmouth, 85th Battalion, who is here tonight; Wallace Pleasant, Toronto, No. 2 Construction Battalion, who is represented by his daughter Mrs. Blanche Evans of Toronto; Percy Richards from Saint John, N.B., who is with us tonight, No. 2 Construction Battalion; Robert Shepard, New Glasgow, No. 2 Construction Battalion; John Smith, Middleton, N.S., No. 2 Construction Battalion, who also served in World War II.

A. Seymour Tyler, who is at my right hand, from Lakeville Corner, Sunbury County, N.B., served with the No. 2 Construction Battalion, as did many of the others; then in 1939 he went overseas in the Second World War with the Carleton and York Regiment; Alfred West of Montreal, Canadian Forestry Corps; Gordon Charles Wilson of Halifax, N.S., who is with us tonight, enlisted in No. 2 it is said at the age of seventeen. A deacon of the Cornwallis Street Baptist Church, former president of the Nova Scotia Association for the Advancement of Coloured People. These are your valiant men, the twenty-one survivors whom we honour in this most fitting manner tonight. So tonight in company with the Secretary of State of Canada, on behalf of the Government of our province, on behalf of our 847,000 people, we ask, in our own way, to be forgiven for having overlooked your contribution. But, alas, we have had our eyes opened and see more deeply than we have ever seen before, with what valour, what brotherhood, and with what hope our Black brothers helped to purchase our freedom.

On your behalf and on behalf of a grateful province, to these veterans, brothers, whose blood is the same colour as my blood, who were prepared to give it, who served and fought, who lived and who dwelled among us. Ring out brave trumpets, sing out proud province, honour Black men of valour, as they wait for the sounding of the trumpet upon the other side.

Ruth Johnson, Program Chairperson, Black Cultural Society, thanked Morris for his stirring and thought-provoking address. The soloists for the evening, Yvonne White and Fred R. Wilson, then combined their talents for a thrilling rendition of the theme song of the Civil Rights Movement, "We Shall Overcome." Following brief remarks by veterans Gordon Charles Wilson, Sydney Morgan Jones, A. Seymour Tyler and Isaac Phills, all of the veterans were presented with certificates of honour. After closing remarks by H. A. J. Wedderburn, the Reunion and Recognition Banquet, an unforgettable evening, wound down with some dancing to the sounds of the Stadacona Band.

The weekend's other activities were as memorable as the Banquet. On Saturday morning (November 13), the veterans were taken on a tour of some Halifax sights, including the Canadian Forces Base, the Fairview Container Pier and Citadel Hill. On Saturday evening, the veterans, their wives and guests attended a reception at the Lord Nelson Hotel sponsored by the Province of Nova Scotia and hosted by the Black Cultural Society. Edmund Morris attended this event as well and, again, an enjoyable time was had by all. On Sunday (November 14), a service at the Cherry Brook Baptist Church, Halifax County, provided a fine end to a momentous weekend.

PEN SKETCHES
AND WAR MEMOIRS

Lieutenant-Colonel Daniel Hugh Sutherland

Lieutenant-Colonel Daniel Hugh Sutherland (1878-1977), a native of River John, Pictou County, N.S., was a veteran of both World Wars. His military career began in 1916, when he enlisted in the 193rd Battalion, CEF, under the command of Lieutenant-Colonel John Stanfield.

On July 5, 1916, he was appointed Commanding Officer of the No. 2 Construction Battalion, CEF, whose headquarters were first located in Pictou, N.S. Sutherland was proud of the Battalion's service in Canada and France.

During World War II, he was called on to organize the 2nd Battalion, Pictou Highlanders. Because of his age (sixty-one), however, he was unable to serve overseas.

Sutherland had a long and fulfilling career. After attending high school in River John, he studied engineering at McGill University in Montreal. He was involved in railroad, dam and road construction for a number of years. During his lifetime, he participated in many worthwhile endeavours that benefited his community, county and province. He was involved in political, hospital, boards-of-trade and church activities.

The Reverend Captain William A. White

The Reverend Captain William A. White was a native of Williamsburg, Va. He came to Nova Scotia in 1899 to study at Acadia University in Wolfville, where he obtained his Bachelor of Arts and Bachelor of Divinity. The outbreak of war in 1914 found White ministering at the Zion Baptist Church in Truro.

It is reported that White was preparing to join the 106th Battalion, CEF, as a private when he received word that the Army planned to authorize a Black battalion. White enlisted and, on February 1, 1917, was taken on as Chaplain of the No. 2 Construction Battalion. He held the rank of Honorary Captain, and he is reported to have been the only Black commissioned officer in the British Armed Forces during World War I.

The nominal roll of the No. 2 Construction Battalion indicates that White served in the Canadian Militia prior to joining the

Battalion. He went overseas with the Battalion and served in England and France.

In 1919, following his service overseas, White returned to Canada and then became Pastor of the Cornwallis Street Baptist Church in Halifax. In May 1936, he became the first Black Canadian to receive an honorary degree, a doctorate of divinity, which was awarded by his Alma Mater, Acadia University. He passed away in September 1936.

Private William Carter

William Carter is believed to be the last surviving veteran of the No. 2 Construction Battalion from the Halifax area. He enlisted in the Battalion on August 7, 1916, at the age of twenty.

Carter was one of the men selected to remove steel rails from the Grand Trunk Railway sidings in New Brunswick for shipment overseas. He received an arm injury during that duty, and on May 18, 1917, after a period of hospitalization, he was discharged as medically unfit.

Carter did not attempt to enlist prior to the formation of No. 2 because they were not taking Blacks in the Army at that time. Bill Kellum and Walter Johnson, he recalled, were recruiting for No. 2, and they convinced him to join.

Carter was stationed at Pictou and Truro before going to Aldershot, N.S., where he took a non-commissioned officer's course. Others from the Battalion on the same course included Bill Kellum, Halifax; Bob Bushfan, Saint John, N.B.; and George Pilgrim and John Clarke, Sydney, N.S. Looking back on his brief army career, Carter recalled:

I got along very good in the Army. The time we spent in New Brunswick was rather rough. It was very cold. In Truro, we had a problem at the theatre. They told us we could not sit downstairs. That was the custom: Blacks had to all go upstairs in the balcony. The boys got that little matter cleared up in a hurry. We had no trouble after that. I have no regrets.

Carter spoke highly of the Commanding Officer, Lieutenant-Colonel Sutherland, and the Chaplain, the Reverend Captain White. Describing Sergeant Sealy, he said:

Sergeant Sealy was a tough, no-nonsense non-commissioned officer. He made you toe the mark, but he was a first-class soldier. I understand that he had served in the British Army. I feel that if he had been a white man, they probably would have made him a commissioned officer.

Private James Elmer Cromwell

James Elmer Cromwell is a native of Southville, Digby County, N.S., and he still resides in that small rural community. He enlisted in the No. 2 Construction Battalion at Truro on October 13, 1916. "I was only sixteen years old when I joined up," he said, "but I told them I was eighteen. I wanted to go with the rest of the boys."

The muster roll indicates that seven Cromwells from the Digby area enlisted in the Battalion. A cousin, Arthur Benson Cromwell, died overseas at the age of nineteen. His name is inscribed on the war memorial in Weymouth, N.S.

With obvious pride and satisfaction, Cromwell recalled his military service: "It definitely was a satisfying experience. I would not have missed it for anything, and I certainly would do it again if I had to. Once you got in the Army, you learned to take care of yourself. You grew up in a hurry."

Cromwell said that, when the No. 2 Construction Battalion arrived overseas, it was trained and fully equipped for battle. Some members of the Battalion saw action with other units, some were wounded, and some died. He said many were disappointed because they were not afforded the opportunity to engage in front-line duty.

Private A. Benjamin Elms

A. Benjamin Elms was a resident of Monastery, Antigonish County, N.S. He enlisted in the No. 2 Construction Battalion at Truro on August 8, 1916. "It was my first attempt to join up," he said.

Elms was employed in the lumber industry prior to joining the Army. "My people had moved to Truro," he recalled. "My cousin Fred was there living on Foundry Hill. He had joined the Army. I decided to join up with him."

Initially, Elms was stationed at Pictou, and later the Battalion moved to Truro. "The officers were all white," he said, "except the Chaplain, Rev. White. He was coloured and came from Truro. I believe that he was born in the States."

Elms believed that some Blacks from the Antigonish-Guysborough area had been accepted into the Army before the No. 2 Construction Battalion was formed. "The 106th Battalion had quite a few coloured boys," he recalled, "including Tom and Sid Jones from Truro."

Elms was nineteen when he enlisted, "right in the prime of life. I did not like army life at first. It was okay overseas, but here in Canada it was miserable, no good. The corporals and sergeants gave you no chance at all."

Elms went overseas with the Battalion in March 1917 and was attached to the Canadian Forestry Corps, CEF, in France. "We worked with the Forestry Corps in the woods," he recalled, "loading lumber and shipping it up to the front lines. We had two or three mills going, night and day. I preferred working with the night crew. The meals were better at night."

Elms had fond memories of the French people. "They were different from the people here in Canada," he said. "They treated us with respect."

Elms himself was not involved in the riot that occurred in Wales while the Battalion was waiting to return home. But he did have some opinions on what led up to the confrontation: "A white soldier made a racial remark, and old Sergeant Sealy ordered his men to put him in the guard house. His buddies came to release him, and all hell broke loose."

When Elms returned to Canada after the War, he went back to the lumber business. He died on February 10, 1984. He was eighty-six.

Private William F. Guy

William F. Guy, a native of Clementsport, Annapolis County, N.S., resided in Kentville, Kings County, before he died on January 11, 1984, at the age of eighty-eight. He was working at a sugar refinery in Saint John when World War I erupted.

Guy tried to sign up in New Brunswick, but was sent back to Nova Scotia, where he was rejected on medical grounds:

I finally got into the Army in 1918. My friend Herby Burchell and I travelled by horse and team from Clementsport to Annapolis Royal, and we were both accepted. . . . We knew what we had to do. We did not think about it; we were ready to fight. We were fighting for our country, Canada, to save it for your parents and for your people to have a country to live in. I never expected to come back.

After receiving his training, Guy sailed from Pier 2 in Halifax aboard the *Nellor*, arriving in England shortly before the War ended. Guy vividly described the scene when it was announced that the War was over:

We were all lined up on the parade ground ready to march off to the boat for France. The Colonel rode down on horseback with a white paper in his hand. The Sergeant brought us to attention. The Colonel said, "Boys the War is over." It was the 11th day of November 1918. I remember that like it was yesterday. I can see it all now, see the Colonel, see the parade ground, see all of the fellows lined up, just like a vision. . . . We were in a mixed unit of approximately two hundred whites and Blacks, trained and ready to go.

With a gleam in his eyes, Guy said proudly, "I truly enjoyed my time in the Army. I liked it so much I tried to enlist again in World War II. They would not take me; they said I was too old."

Private Sydney Morgan Jones

A native of Truro, Sydney Morgan Jones has been a long-time resident of Halifax. He serves as Chairman of the Board of Deacons, Cornwallis Street Baptist Church, and he also manages the Age and Opportunity Centre of that church.

Jones enlisted in the 106th Battalion on June 3, 1916, shortly after his fifteenth birthday. He trained at Truro and left Halifax for overseas duty on July 15, 1916, aboard the SS *Empress of Britain*. Jones said he did not encounter a great deal of racism while serving in the 106th Battalion, although some white soldiers resented the presence of Blacks in the unit.

As a boy, Jones was impressed by the sight of thousands of soldiers passing through Truro on the troop trains, *en route* to Halifax and Europe. He turned fifteen in May, dropped out of school and enlisted in June:

I thought it would be a good idea to join the Forces, to see what was happening. We were meeting all the troop trains, shaking hands with them, wishing them luck and all that sort of thing. I guess it looked like the thing to do, to be a soldier. I sort of got caught up in the spirit of the thing.

On arrival in England, the 106th Battalion was broken up into reinforcements for other units. Jones himself was assigned to one of this country's oldest and most famous combat units, the Royal Canadian Regiment, CEF, which has earned battle honours in the Boer War, World War I, World War II and the Korean War. Jones described the break-up of the 106th and his transfer to the Regiment:

There was some feeling of disappointment among the boys when the 106th was broken up. However, we did not mind it too much. There is no point in minding things that you cannot help. We were there to follow orders. When we joined the Royal Canadian Regiment in the trenches, it had been under fire for some time. I had no problems. It welcomed anybody, whether you were Black, white or whatever colour you were.

Jones said his uncle Jeremiah (Jerry) Jones had also been drafted from the 106th to the Royal Canadian Regiment:

Uncle Jerry wiped out a German machine-gun nest during action at Vimy Ridge, was recommended for a Distinguished Conduct Medal, but did not receive it. . . . Not too many people are aware that Blacks fought and died overseas. It was the same situation as William Hall, VC. Many people, both Black and white, were unaware that William Hall, who won the Victoria Cross, was a Black man, a Black Nova Scotian.

Jones served with the Royal Canadian Regiment until he was wounded at Passendale, Belgium, on October 30, 1917. He recuperated at Camp Hill Hospital in Halifax until he was discharged from the Army in July 1919. "It was quite an experience, indeed it was," Jones said about his military service. "Looking back now, I would not have missed it for anything."

Seaman John R. Pannill

A long-standing resident of Halifax, John R. Pannill was born in Yarmouth, N.S., in 1898. He is a member of the Cornwallis Street Baptist Church and has served on its board of deacons.

Pannill was a merchant seaman during World War I, when he was about seventeen. He visited a number of places in the British Isles, including London and Liverpool. Prior to becoming a merchant seaman, he had volunteered for service in the Canadian Army. "I was living in Halifax at the time," he recalled, "and I decided to join the Army. I went to the Armouries and inquired. The recruiting officer informed me that I could not enlist because they were not taking Black fellows."

Pannill left the Armouries, went down to the shipping office and had no problem signing up as a seaman. He worked in the engine room as a fireman on the boilers and sometimes as an oiler. The ship's crew, "a pretty rough and fearless group," consisted of men from all over the world.

Pannill remembered life as a wartime seaman as "pretty good," although it was dangerous due to German submarines. The ships sailed at night under the protection of warships.

After his wartime service ended, Pannill remained in Halifax, where he secured employment with the Canadian National Railway as a sleeping-car porter. He was later promoted to Porter-in-Charge. He retired from the CNR on October 10, 1972, with more than forty-three years of continuous service to his credit.

Acting Corporal Isaac Phills

Isaac Phills was a native of St. Vincent, a small island in the West Indies. He was a resident of Sydney, N.S., for more than sixty years, before moving to Dartmouth, N.S.

In 1967, he was awarded the Order of Canada for outstanding citizenship, for providing university and vocational education for his seven children. He is reported to have been the first Black to receive the Order of Canada.

Phills substantiated the fact that, during the early years of World War I, Blacks had difficulty joining the Canadian Army. He also pointed out, however, that, when conscription became the law of the land, Blacks were subjected to the call-up process along with whites.

After he was drafted in 1918, he received his initial training at Aldershot. He recalled that, while stationed in Canada, Black and white soldiers were fully integrated. On arrival in England, however, the approximately sixty Black soldiers were placed in a segregated unit:

In Canada, we experienced no problems. The training and living conditions were on an integrated basis. We trained, ate and lived together. We sailed for overseas together as Canadian soldiers. Shortly after arriving in England, we were taken out of the regular group we had trained with and put by ourselves. We did not ask why; we just followed orders.

Phills was appointed Acting Corporal of his small segregated unit. Although trained for combat duty, the unit was assigned to fatigue and labour duties. Before it completed its training, the Armistice was signed. The unit was then sent to a camp in Rhyl, Wales. While stationed in Rhyl, Phills met some members of the No. 2 Construction Battalion, which was on its way back to Canada from France.

After he completed his military service, Phills returned to Sydney and his job at the steel plant. He died on March 9, 1985.

Private Wallace James Pleasant

Wallace James Pleasant was a native of Weymouth Falls, Digby County. The World War I veteran last resided at the Veteran's Pavilion, Sunnybrook Hospital, Toronto.

Pleasant was twenty-four years old when he enlisted in the No. 2 Construction Battalion on July 27, 1916. He trained at Pictou and Truro before going to England and France. Pleasant was attached to the Forestry Corps, and at one time, he was batman to Lieutenant-Colonel Daniel Hugh Sutherland.

After his discharge from the Army, Pleasant was employed on coal boats in Halifax. He also worked in Boston, Mass., for approximately eighteen years.

Due to health reasons, Pleasant was unable to attend the Reunion and Recognition Weekend. He was represented by his daughter Blanche Evans, of Toronto. He passed away on October 12, 1984.

Private Percy J. Richards

Percy J. Richards is a native of Saint John, where he still resides.
Richards enlisted in the No. 2 Construction Battalion at Saint
John on August 10, 1916, at the age of twenty-one. He served
at Pictou and Truro before embarking from Halifax for overseas
service. Richards recalled his unsuccessful attempts to enlist in
the Army prior to the authorization of the Battalion:

*We would go to the recruiting centre in Sussex. I went there with
some friends several times. The recruitment officer, who was of German
descent, told us that it was not a Black man's war. He questioned why
we wanted to join the Army.*

Richards said that, after arriving in England, the Battalion
underwent further training and was segregated from the white
troops. He served in France and Belgium while attached to the
Forestry Corps and was sent to the 21st Battalion, CEF. He served
as the bugler of that unit until the War ended.

Richards was discharged from the Army in February 1919. Afterwards, he went to work at the Atlantic Sugar Refinery, where
he was employed for thirty-nine years.

Private Robert Shepard

Robert Shepard was born near Mulgrave, Guysborough County, N.S., and he moved to New Glasgow, N.S., in 1912. He enlisted in the No. 2 Construction Battalion on August 10, 1916. After completing military training at Pictou and Truro, he embarked for overseas service on March 28, 1917. He said that a number of "the boys" volunteered their services before 1916, but were not accepted:

A group came up from Sydney to enlist. West Indian boys and some Canadians, about fifty all together. They went in there in the morning on the first train. They stayed until five p.m. Finally, they were told, "This is not for you fellows; this is a white man's war. When we want you we will send for you." Some of the boys vowed never to volunteer again.

Shepard noted that, when things "got so hot" in France, the authorities decided to accept Blacks, opening up the recruiting stations and forming a Black battalion. Récruits for No. 2 came from all over the province, different parts of the country and even the United States.

During his stay overseas, Shepard performed various duties. For a while, he was assigned to a field hospital, where he helped move and prepare the dead for burial. Shepard vividly recalled the riot that broke out after the Armistice. It occurred at Kimmel Park, North Wales, and involved soldiers from his battalion and another unit:

No. 2 was on bath parade under the direction of Sergeant Sealy. A sergeant-major from another unit ignored orders from Sergeant Sealy and interfered with the line of march. When he was arrested, some of his comrades attempted to remove him from the guard house. A riot broke out, and a number of soldiers ended up in the hospital.

Due to ill health, Shepard was unable to attend the Reunion and Recognition Weekend. He passed away on April 19, 1983, at the age of ninety.

Sergeant Charles Nathan Smith

The Reverend Charles Nathan Smith (Sergeant) was born in Birchtown, Shelburne County, N.S. He was ordained as a Pentecostal minister in 1929, and he was the Pastor of the Sharon Assembly Church in Yarmouth for more than thirty years. He also served congregations in Shelburne and Amherst, N.S., and Woodstock, N.B.

Prior to becoming an ordained minister, Smith served in the No. 2 Construction Battalion, in which he enlisted at Truro on September 4, 1916. He held the rank of Sergeant and also served as Acting Regimental Sergeant-Major.

Concerning the rationale behind the authorization of a segregated battalion, Smith said, "No. 2 Battalion was formed due to discrimination and prejudice. The policy of the Army, official or otherwise, was not to accept Black volunteers into the regular units."

According to Smith, members of the Battalion encountered some prejudice in France, where American servicemen had spread rumours concerning Black soldiers. He noted as well that the Battalion came under fire in France from German air raids.

Smith passed away on December 15, 1973, two years after he was interviewed.

Private John Smith

John Smith is a native of Hants County currently residing in Middleton, N.S. He saw service in both World Wars.

On September 4, 1916, at the age of sixteen, Smith enlisted in the No. 2 Construction Battalion at Windsor, N.S. Like other battalion members, he received his military training at Pictou and Truro before going overseas. "We were stationed near the Swiss border," he said. "We did logging work, getting out the logs for railroad tracks, bridges and the trenches. At times, it was pretty good; at other times, it was pretty bad and pretty lonely."

Smith joined the No. 2 Construction Battalion because he wanted "to be with the boys from the Windsor area," who had been his co-workers in the gypsum quarry. He said a number of men from Annapolis Valley communities enlisted in the Battalion, including Cornelius (Neil) and Harold States, Moses Stevenson, Clarence Allison, Frank Johnson and others.

Smith also served in World War II for about three years as a member of the Veteran's Guard. He was stationed at a prisoner of war camp in Medicine Hat, Alta. "I have no regrets," he said. "My service in both wars was a real learning experience."

Private Richard Stanley Symonds

Richard Stanley Symonds was born in Upper Hammonds Plains, Halifax County. He enlisted in the No. 2 Construction Battalion on December 17, 1916, at the age of seventeen.

Symonds trained at Pictou and Truro before going to Europe. Following the Armistice, he returned to Canada and was discharged from the Army on February 21, 1919.

Symonds served on the Board of Deacons of the Cornwallis Street Baptist Church in Halifax for more than thirty years. He was also Moderator of the African United Baptist Association. Symonds was a founder and long-time supporter of the Nova Scotia Association for the Advancement of Coloured People. He passed away on February 23, 1979.

Sergeant A. Seymour Tyler

A. Seymour Tyler, a veteran of both World Wars, last resided in Lakeville Corner, Sunbury County, N.B., where he augmented his Old Age Pension with income from his farm.

Tyler, a native of Saint John, went overseas in World War I with the No. 2 Construction Battalion. Following the War, he served in the Canadian Militia for approximately thirty years.

When World War II started in 1939, he again answered the call of duty. He went to England in December 1939 as a bugle sergeant in the famed Carleton & York Regiment, 3rd Brigade, 1st Canadian Division. Tyler had the honour of leading his combat regiment ashore when its ship landed. On one occasion, while the troops were being reviewed, both King George VI (shown above) and Queen Elizabeth II engaged him in brief conversations. Concerning Black soldiers, Tyler remarked:

Do not let anyone tell you different, no man is any braver than a Black man. He has everything that it takes, and he has proven it, although he has not received recognition for his courage. After all, the Black man went over there, he trained like a soldier, he fought like a soldier and died like a soldier, and that is all any white man can do.

Tyler said that his World War I exploits included service with the 8th Winnipeg Rifles, CEF, as well as action at Vimy Ridge and Passendale. He displayed a strong sense of devotion to military service. "If I were a young man today," he said, "I would be right back in the Army."

Following his discharge from the Army at the end of World War II, Tyler was employed by the Canadian Pacific Railway as a sleeping-car porter, a position he held for twenty-five years. He died on February 17, 1985, at the age of eighty-seven.

Private Gordon Charles Wilson

Gordon Charles Wilson was born in Upper Hammonds Plains, a rural Black community located approximately twenty miles north-west of Halifax. He was a long-time resident of Halifax and played an active role in church, Canadian Legion and other community activities.

Wilson, with his clear memory, graphically recalled that, when the War broke out in 1914, his brother immediately went to the recruiting station in Halifax, where he was told, "Mister, this is a white man's war. When we want you, we will let you know." Wilson said his brother was extremely disappointed and, consequently, made no further attempt to enlist in the Canadian Army.

Wilson himself enlisted in the No. 2 Construction Battalion at the age of seventeen (he lied about his age) on September 2, 1916. He trained at Pictou and Truro before embarking for overseas duty on March 28, 1917. Wilson said the Battalion received the same infantry training as the combat troops. He recalled, as well, that he knew a few Blacks who were accepted into the Army before the Battalion was organized. "Black people refused to accept the attitude that it was 'a white man's war,' " he said. "As loyal citizens, we wanted to serve our country. It was our duty, our responsibility."

Wilson noted that the ten-day trip overseas was rough, especially with enemy submarines on the prowl. He described how a ship in the convoy was hit and sunk not far from the Irish coast.

Wilson's detachment was assigned to the Forestry Corps, and he served in the Jura Mountains and in Marseilles in southern France. While on leave, he visited London, Edinburgh and a number of other major centres. "I have never regretted going into the Army," he said. "I found it a very good adventure, travelling and seeing some of the world. All in all, it was an unforgettable experience. There are not too many of us left."

Wilson passed away on July 4, 1983, at the age of eighty-four.

Private William Henry Bundy, Cherry Brook, Halifax County, N.S., enlisted in the No. 2 Construction Battalion on August 11, 1916, at Amherst, N.S. He passed away on September 13, 1965, at the age of eighty-eight.

Private Henry William Bundy, Cherry Brook, Halifax County, N.S., enlisted in the No. 2 Construction Battalion at Amherst, N.S., on August 11, 1916. He served in Canada, England and France. He died at the age of fifty-one, along with his son Milton and several others, in a tragic fire that destroyed Kays Department Store, Barrington Street, Halifax, N.S., on November 30, 1950.

Private Clayton Thomas Harris, Beechville,
N.S., enlisted in the Canadian Army at the
age of eighteen. He served in Canada and
England. He passed away on June 8, 1979,
at the age of eighty-four.

Private Ottus Farmer, Shelburne, N.S.

Corporal John R. Sparks, Loon Lake , Halifax County, N.S., served in Canada and England. He died on May 2, 1964.

The late Private Moses Stevenson, Thorne's Cove, Annapolis County, N.S., enlisted in the No. 2 Construction Battalion on December 30, 1916.

Private William Winslow Paris (left), Mulgrave, N.S.; Private George William Reddick, New Glasgow, N.S. Both served in the No. 2 Construction Battalion.

World War I veterans in London, England. Front row centre: Private Joseph Alexander Paris, No. 2 Construction Battalion; enlisted on July 25, 1916. Other soldiers are unidentified.

The late Private James Aubrey Cromwell (left) and Private James Elmer Cromwell, Southville, Digby County, N.S. enlisted in the No. 2 Construction Battalion on October 13, 1916.

Private Arthur Benson Cromwell, Weymouth Falls, Digby County, N.S., No. 2 Construction Battalion, died in April 1917 while *en route* to England.

Private Wesley Parsons, Lucasville, Halifax County, N.S., died on April 14, 1977.

Private Edward (Ned) Brown, Dartmouth, N.S., passed away in 1945.

SYNOPSIS

At the outbreak of World War I, Black men, like their white brothers, were eager to bear arms. They, too, were caught up in the excitement, the enthusiasm and the patriotism surrounding the War, which was grandiosely acclaimed as "the war to end all wars," "a war to make the world safe for democracy."

It was both an emotional time and a majestic time, a time for one's manhood to be tested in the arena of world conflict. Men and boys alike streamed to the recruiting centres, and from there, to training camps and the battlefields of Europe.

Some volunteers sought the glory, the adventure, the status and the financial benefits associated with the King's uniform. Blacks wanted to share in the action as well. In the words of veteran Sydney Morgan Jones, "It was the thing to do."[1]

It was not a simple and straightforward process for Blacks, however. They had to fight for the right to serve King and Country, as many commanding and recruiting officers refused to accept Blacks into their units. Consequently, the first battle Blacks had to fight was not on the front lines overseas, but on native soil at home.

In 1938 — under the authority of the Minister of National Defence — Colonel A. Fortescue Duguid, Director of the Historical Section, General Staff, wrote the official history of the Canadian Forces in the Great War. In his 596-page work, the author tersely described Black enlistment in four words: "Black volunteers were refused."[2]

By contrast, other minority groups did not experience the same problems. Canada's Indians, for example, were accepted by the hundreds into front-line combat battalions.[3] Indeed, some light-skinned Blacks evaded "the colour bar" by passing for Indian or white men.[4]

In response to the prevailing prejudice, Black leaders and citizens, such as the Reverend Captain William A. White and Samuel Reese, both of Truro, N.S., George Morton of Hamilton, Ont.,

Members of the William Hall, VC, Branch of the Royal Canadian Legion parade on the grounds of the old Joseph Howe School in Halifax c1945. World War I veterans include William Henry Bundy, Walter A. Johnson, Alexander Brammah, Harold Coleman Tabb, Louis Middleton, William R. Johnson, Harold States, Richard Stanley Symonds and Samuel Turner. World War II veterans include Willie Medley, Wendell Skeir, Bill Johnson and Barrington Howe. Others are unidentified.

John T. Richards of Saint John, N.B., and J. R. B. Whitney of Toronto, Ont., made the rejection of Black volunteers a national issue. They publicized the frustration and humiliation felt by Blacks, and they requested that Black men be accorded the same military rights as white men—the right to serve, to shed their blood and to die if necessary. Their patriotic pleas for equality stirred the conscierce of a nation engaged in a life-and-death struggle to preserve democratic ideals and principles. The hypocrisy inherent in the blatant discriminatory rejection of Black volunteers could not be ignored indefinitely.

Finally, in April 1916, in a belated response to Black protests and after some embarrassing queries in the House of Commons, the Chief of the General Staff, Major-General W. G. Gwatkin, recommended the formation of one or more Black labour battalions. The unit designated for Black volunteers was the No. 2 Construction Battalion, CEF. Black hopes became a reality nearly two years after the outbreak of the War, which had already seen thousands of Canadian casualties.

Despite the previous rejections and despite the segregated status of the Battalion, hundreds of Black Canadians quickly took advantage of the opportunity to enlist. As in previous wars, they were prepared to serve in any capacity.

Private Byron Hatfield Tynes, Dartmouth, N.S., enlisted in the No. 2 Construction Battalion on January 4, 1917. He passed away on December 10, 1963.

James Frederick Tynes, Dartmouth, N.S., No. 2 Construction Battalion, passed away in 1970 at the age of eighty-two.

Following the signing of the Armistice on November 11, 1918, Black soldiers were sent home. They returned, without fanfare, to their homes in cities, towns and villages across the country—from Cape Breton Island in the East to Vancouver Island in the West. Some Blacks re-established themselves in historic Black communities such as Tracadie, N.S., Buxton, Ont., and Saltspring Island, B.C.

The Black Americans in the unit, meanwhile, were dispatched to their homes in the United States. Some returned to cities and towns in the Deep South, such as Montgomery, Ala., Shreveport, La., and Oxford, Miss., places that later gained international prominence during the highly publicized civil rights movement of the sixties.

In Nova Scotia, veterans such as Ernest Grosse of Dartmouth, Harold Simmonds of Kentville and Edward Sealy of Halifax became sleeping-car porters for the Canadian National Railway. Other veterans, such as William Wesley of New Edinburgh and A. Benjamin Elms of Truro, took up farming and lumbering.

Charles Nathan Smith of Yarmouth became a Pentecostal minister, and Adolphus F. Skinner of Halifax became a Methodist and, later, a Baptist preacher. Both served as pastors in Nova Scotia and New Brunswick for more than thirty years. Skinner also served as the Moderator of the African United Baptist Asso-

Arthur Stevens (left) Greenville, Yarmouth County, N.S., enlisted in the No. 2 Construction Battalion on August 8, 1916. Chester Pannill, Yarmouth, N.S., enlisted in the Battalion on August 26, 1916. Both are deceased; Pannill died while *en route* overseas.

ciation, the oldest and largest Black organization in Nova Scotia. Gordon Charles Wilson and Richard Stanley Symonds of Upper Hammonds Plains, Byron H. Tynes of Dartmouth, Sydney Morgan Jones of Truro, William Barton of Acaciaville and several others also answered the call of Christian leadership. They were ordained as deacons in African United Baptist churches.

A number of the returning soldiers saw secular organizations as another means of acquiring a better life-style for Blacks. Walter A. Johnson of Halifax, for example, was one of the organizers of the William Hall, VC, Branch of the Royal Canadian Legion. Isaac Phills of Sydney provided leadership in the Ancient Order of Foresters and the Ethiopian Community Club.

In any event, the Blacks who were prepared to serve and die in the defence of freedom came home to many of the same restrictions they had left behind. The Great War did not end all wars, it did not make the world safe for democracy, and it did not signal an end to racial prejudice. Blacks were still subjected to segregated housing, segregated employment and even some segregated graveyards.[5]

Some Black soldiers did not return from the War at all. The Nova Scotia honour roll of those who died overseas included John Lambert of Halifax, Arthur Benson Cromwell and Reuben Alexander Smith of Weymouth Falls, Chester Pannill and Percy Berryman of Yarmouth, Rollie and Norman Ash of Antigonish, Ralph Leslie Stoutley of Truro, Nathaniel Steward of East Preston and many others.

During the early years of World War II, Black volunteers again experienced problems with enlistment. In one instance, a group of experienced Black seamen who volunteered for service in the Navy was not accepted because it wasn't large enough to form an entire crew. Segregation, therefore, was still the prevailing attitude in the Navy. Lee Carvery, a resident of Dartmouth who served with the Canadian Army during World War II, recalled his unsuccessful attempt to enlist in the Navy:

I was one of a large group of Blacks who had gone to sea prior to World War II. When the War started, based on our experience, about fifteen of us decided to join the Navy. After passing the medical examination, we were informed by letter that, if enough Blacks came forward to man a ship, we would be accepted into the Navy.[6]

A small number of Blacks did, however, serve in the Navy and Air Force. In Dartmouth, Allan Bundy, then a university student, was accepted by the Air Force in 1943 after being rejected on racial grounds four years earlier. He attributed his accep-

Private William H. Barton, Acaciaville, Digby County, N.S., served with the 25th Battalion. He died on May 11, 1973, at the age of eighty-five.

The late Private George E. Downey, Halifax, N.S., enlisted in the No. 2 Construction Battalion on September 1, 1916. He also served in World War II as a member of the Veteran's Guard.

tance to a change in commanding officers at the Halifax recruiting station.[7] Bundy became the first, and probably the only, Black Nova Scotian to be accepted for air-crew training. He completed forty-two missions while serving overseas, and at the time of his discharge in 1946, he held the rank of Flying Officer.

By 1941, as the War intensified, Black volunteers were being accepted into the Army in substantial numbers. By the end of the War in 1945, several thousands were serving in various branches of the Army. In short, there was some progress in World War II: no segregated Black battalion was authorized; Black servicemen were integrated into military units. Segregation was out, integration was in. As well, several Blacks received commendations for bravery and conduct.

In World War I, the Reverend Captain William A. White was the only Black commissioned officer in the British Empire. In World War II, a number of Black servicemen received commissions in the Army and Air Force. For example, on February 1, 1944, the Reverend W. P. Oliver, the Pastor of Cornwallis Street Baptist Church in Halifax, was made a chaplain and a captain in the Canadian Army. Attached to Headquarters Staff, Military

Private William I. Clements, Bridgetown, N.S., a veteran of both World Wars.

District 6, Canadian Chaplaincy Pool, he was responsible for the religious needs of Black servicemen in the Army, Navy and Air Force.

The involvement, status and acceptance of Black servicemen in the Canadian military establishment has come a long way since the third-class days of World War I. There was, after all, some light at the end of a long, dark tunnel. Now, a considerable number of Black officers and enlisted men are serving in all branches of the Armed Forces.

EPILOGUE

The ranks of Black World War I veterans have all but disappeared. From late 1982 to 1986, the last post sounded for Robert Shepard of New Glasgow, N.S., Gordon Charles Wilson and Albert David Deleon of Halifax, N.S., A. Benjamin Elms of Monastery, N.S., William Forest Guy of Kentville, N.S., Wallace Pleasant of Toronto, Ont., George W. Harrison and Alfred West of Montreal, Que., A. Seymour Tyler of Lakeville Corner, N.B., Isaac Phills of Dartmouth, N.S., and John Wesley Hamilton of Verdun, Que.

The Halifax-Dartmouth vicinity alone saw eighty-five volunteers join the ranks of the No. 2 Construction Battalion, CEF. In mid-1987, William Carter was the only survivor of that group. Western Nova Scotia, too, sent some eighty-five men to the Battalion, of whom only John Smith, James Elmer Cromwell and Malcolm Jarvis remained in mid-1987.

At that time, there were still some Black survivors of other units. For example, Sydney Morgan Jones, of the 106th Battalion, CEF, was active in Halifax's Cornwallis Street Baptist Church.

The Black Cultural Society's Reunion and Recognition Banquet in November 1982 gave these and other Black veterans a richly deserved legacy that attracted national attention. On November 14, 1982, Alan Story wrote in the Toronto *Star:*

They dug trenches, built bridges and defused land mines for Canada in World War I. They faced mustard gas like other soldiers. But the No. 2 Construction Battalion, Canadian Expeditionary Force, the only battalion of Black Canadians to serve in the "war to end all wars," never received its share of the glory.[1]

Perhaps the late A. Seymour Tyler, a veteran of both World Wars, best described the significance of the Banquet. "The Black Cultural Society," he said, "has resurrected the unknown and forgotten soldiers of the Great War."[2] Edmund Morris, the Nova Scotia Minister of Social Services, also commented on the events: "Alas, we have had our eyes opened and see more deeply than

The Tyler brothers, Saint John, N.B., veterans of both World Wars. Seated is Sergeant A. Seymour; standing is Private Charles E. They both served in the No. 2 Construction Battalion.

we have ever seen before, with what valour, what brotherhood, and with what hope our Black brothers helped to purchase our freedom."[3]

The authorization on July 5, 1916, of a segregated Black battalion exposed the latent prejudice in this country. In all likelihood, such a discriminatory policy shall never again be repeated. The Human Rights Act of the late seventies and, more recently, the Charter of Rights and Freedoms, which prohibit discrimination based on race, colour, etc., apply to all facets of Canadian society, including the Armed Forces.

It is hoped that this modest book will, in some small way, lead to a better understanding of Black contributions to Canadian military history. Perhaps it will inspire others to delve further into the Black heritage above the 49th Parallel.

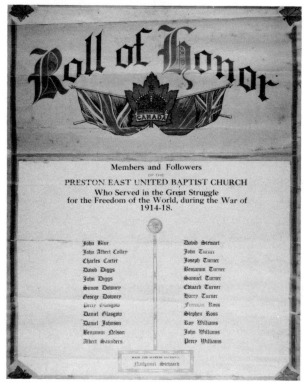

The Roll of Honor at the East Preston United Baptist Church, East Preston, N.S.

APPENDIX A

No. 2 Construction Battalion, CEF

Cape Breton Island	Sgt.-Maj.	Alberga, George Frederick	Sydney, N.S.
	Pte.	Bailey, John	Sydney, N.S.
	Pte.	Bowers, Edward	Sydney, N.S.
	Pte.	Bowers, Frank	Glace Bay, N.S.
	Pte.	Brammah, Alexander	Sydney, N.S.
	Pte.	Brown, George Deane	Sydney, N.S.
	Pte.	Butcher, Leonard Walter	Sydney, N.S.
	Pte.	Byer, Lloyd	Sydney, N.S.
	Pte.	Clarke, John	Sydney, N.S.
	Pte.	Collymore, Grandville	Sydney, N.S.
	Pte.	Cox, Garnet Wesley	Sydney, N.S.
	Pte.	Darlington, Adolphus	Glace Bay, N.S.
	Pte.	Dottin, Joseph	Sydney, N.S.
	Sgt.	Edwards, Matthew Nathaniel	Sydney, N.S.
	Corp.	Flood, Sydney	Sydney, N.S.
	Pte.	Fordingham, Joseph	Sydney, N.S.
	Pte.	Griffiths, Henry	Sydney, N.S.
	Pte.	Hall, Belfield	Sydney, N.S.
	Pte.	Hall, Da Costa	Sydney, N.S.
	Pte.	Harris, Joseph	Sydney, N.S.
	Corp.	Henry, Frederick	New Waterford, N.S.
	Pte.	Horton, Charles	Sydney, N.S.
	Pte.	Jackson, Michael	Glace Bay, N.S.
	Pte.	James, Gilbert	Sydney, N.S.
	Pte.	King, David	Sydney, N.S.
	Pte.	Kirton, Evan	Sydney, N.S.
	Corp.	Medford, Walter	Sydney, N.S.
	Pte.	Miller, Charles	Sydney, N.S.
	Pte.	Montague, Thomas	Sydney, N.S.
	Pte.	Nurse, Edmund	Sydney, N.S.
	Pte.	O'Neil, Herbert Arthur	Sydney, N.S.
	Pte.	Parris, Clement	Sydney, N.S.
	Pte.	Pilgrim, George	Sydney, N.S.
	Pte.	Sergeant, Rufus	Sydney, N.S.
	Pte.	Sheppard, Charles	Sydney, N.S.
	Pte.	Stoute, Seifert	Sydney, N.S.
	Pte.	Sullivan, Julian	Sydney, N.S.
	Pte.	Talbot, Angus	Sydney, N.S.
	Pte.	Tarbot, Ernest	Glace Bay, N.S.
	Pte.	Tarbot, George William	Glace Bay, N.S.
	Pte.	Thorne, Arden Rufus	Sydney, N.S.
	Pte.	Waith, Evans	Sydney, N.S.
	Pte.	Whelan, George Alfred	Sydney, N.S.
	Pte.	Williams, Nathaniel	Sydney, N.S.
	Pte.	Young, James	Sydney, N.S.

Antigonish/Colchester/	Lt.-Col.	Sutherland, Daniel Hugh (CO)	River John, N.S.
Guysborough/Pictou	Capt.	Murray, Dan (MO)	Tatamagouche, N.S.
	Capt.	White, William A. (Chaplain)	Truro, N.S.
	Lieut.	Barnhill, Isaac Logan	Truro, N.S.
	Lieut.	MacLean, Herbert Boyne	Pictou, N.S.
	Lieut.	Parker, George Henry	Truro, N.S.
	Pte.	Ash, Clarence	Truro, N.S.
	Pte.	Ash, Thomas	Big Tracadie, N.S.
	Pte.	Backus, John Joseph	Goldenville, N.S.
	Pte.	Borden, David	Truro, N.S.
	Pte.	Borden, George	Goldenville, N.S.
	Pte.	Borden, Thomas	Truro, N.S.
	Pte.	Bowden, Norman	Guysborough, N.S.
	Pte.	Byard, John Arthur	Truro, N.S.
	Pte.	Byard, Percy Lewis	Truro, N.S.
	Pte.	Byard, William Howard	Truro, N.S.
	Pte.	Clyke, Joseph	Guysborough, N.S.
	Pte.	Clyke, Joseph Palmer	Truro, N.S.
	Pte.	Day, Lavin	Big Tracadie, N.S.
	Pte.	Day, Matthew	Big Tracadie, N.S.
	Pte.	Desmond, Harvey	New Glasgow, N.S.
	Pte.	Desmond, Howard	Guysborough, N.S.
	Pte.	Desmond, Isaac	New Glasgow, N.S.
	Pte.	Desmond, James	Guysborough, N.S.
	Pte.	Desmond, John Henry	New Glasgow, N.S.
	Pte.	Elms, A. Benjamin	Truro, N.S.
	Pte.	Elms, Alexander	Tracadie, N.S.
	Pte.	Elms, Frederick Gordon	Truro, N.S.
	Pte.	Elms, John	Big Tracadie, N.S.
	Pte.	Elms, Michael Redmond	Tracadie, N.S.
	Pte.	Elms, Walter Howard	Truro, N.S.
	Pte.	Fee, Ernest	Antigonish, N.S.
	Pte.	Gero, William	Big Tracadie, N.S.
	Pte.	Jackson, Hartley	Guysborough, N.S.
	Pte.	Johnson, Herbert	Truro, N.S.
	Pte.	Johnson, Reuben	Truro, N.S.
	Pte.	Jones, James Arthur	New Glasgow, N.S.
	Pte.	MacLean, Frederick Mansfield	New Glasgow, N.S.
	Pte.	McPhie, Norman	Antigonish, N.S.
	Pte.	Mintus, Horace Francis	Truro, N.S.
	Pte.	Paris, Frank Leslie	Truro, N.S.
	Pte.	Paris, Joseph Alexander	Mulgrave, N.S.
	Pte.	Paris, Thomas Sheldon	Truro, N.S.
	Pte.	Paris, William Lawrence	Truro, N.S.
	Pte.	Paris, William Winslow	Mulgrave, N.S.
	Pte.	Reddick, George William	New Glasgow, N.S.
	Corp.	Reese, Samuel	Truro, N.S.
	Pte.	Reid, Thomas	New Glasgow, N.S.
	Pte.	Shepard, Robert	New Glasgow, N.S.
	Pte.	Smith, William	New Glasgow, N.S.
	Pte.	Smithers, William	New Glasgow, N.S.
	Pte.	Stevens, Arthur	Greenvale, N.S.
	Pte.	Sylvie, George	New Glasgow, N.S.
	Pte.	Talbot, James Alexander	Mulgrave, N.S.
	Pte.	Talbot, James Ivan	Truro, N.S.
	Pte.	Talbot, Wallace	New Glasgow, N.S.
	Pte.	Talbot, William John	Mulgrave, N.S.
	Pte.	Tynes, Harry Henry	Truro, N.S.
	Pte.	Williams, Charles Frederick	Truro, N.S.

Cumberland	Capt.	Anderson, David	Springhill, N.S.
	Corp.	Corbin, Percy	Amherst, N.S.
	Pte.	Jones, William Percy	Amherst, N.S.
	Pte.	Joseph, Robert Russell	Amherst, N.S.
	Pte.	Mallard, Thomas	Amherst, N.S.
	Corp.	Martin, Lawrence	Amherst, N.S.
	Pte.	Martin, Lloyd William	Amherst, N.S.
	QM Sgt.	Peacock, George Stephen	Amherst, N.S.
	Pte.	Tucker, Alfred Gray	Amherst, N.S.
Annapolis/Digby/	Lieut.	Hood, Samuel Clifford	Yarmouth, N.S.
Hants/Kings/Queens/	Pte.	Allison, Clarence	Windsor, N.S.
Shelburne/Yarmouth	Pte.	Allison, Kenneth	Windsor, N.S.
	Pte.	Allison, William	Windsor, N.S.
	Pte.	Atkinson, Henry	Windsor, N.S.
	Corp.	Bell, Kilson Daniel	Shelburne, N.S.
	Pte.	Bennett, Ancil	Shelburne, N.S.
	Pte.	Bennett, Frank	Shelburne, N.S.
	Pte.	Bennett, Harry	Shelburne, N.S.
	Pte.	Berry, Freeman	Yarmouth, N.S.
	Pte.	Berry, Gordon	Yarmouth, N.S.
	Pte.	Berryman, Percy	Yarmouth, N.S.
	Pte.	Butler, Robert Andrew	Liverpool, N.S.
	Pte.	Crawford, Bowman	Yarmouth, N.S.
	Pte.	Cromwell, Arthur Benson	Weymouth Falls, N.S.
	Pte.	Cromwell, Charles Joseph	Danvers, N.S.
	Pte.	Cromwell, James Aubrey	Southville, N.S.
	* Pte.	Cromwell, James Elmer	Southville, N.S.
	Pte.	Cromwell, Joseph Herbert	Southville, N.S.
	Pte.	Cromwell, Joseph Orvie	Southville, N.S.
	Pte.	Cromwell, Nealy	Southville, N.S.
	Pte.	Croxen, James	Windsor, N.S.
	Pte.	Curry, John	Thorne's Cove, N.S.
	Pte.	Daring, William	Shelburne, N.S.
	Pte.	Downey, Clifford	Shelburne, N.S.
	Pte.	Edison, Robert Alexander	Annapolis Royal, N.S.
	Pte.	Farmer, Arthur	Shelburne, N.S.
	Pte.	Farmer, Harmon Elison	Shelburne, N.S.
	Pte.	Farmer, Zachariah	Shelburne, N.S.
	Pte.	Francis, Charles	Digby, N.S.
	Pte.	Francis, Charles Edward	Annapolis Royal, N.S.
	Pte.	Francis, Luke	Digby, N.S.
	Pte.	Grey, Everett	Windsor, N.S.
	Pte.	Hamilton, Benjamin	Windsor, N.S.
	Pte.	Hamilton, John Wesley	Windsor, N.S.
	Pte.	Hamilton, Prescott Hilton	Windsor, N.S.
	Pte.	Harris, Omer	Kentville, N.S.
	Pte.	Irving, Leonard	Acaciaville, N.S.
	Pte.	Irving, Robert Fenuel	Annapolis Royal, N.S.
	Pte.	Jacklin, Charles Alfred	Shelburne, N.S.
	Pte.	Jacklin, Douglas	Shelburne, N.S.
	Pte.	Jacklin, William Hastings	Shelburne, N.S.
	Pte.	Jackson, Charles Leonard	Hillaton, N.S.
	Pte.	Jackson, Lawrence	Bridgetown, N.S.
	Pte.	Jackson, Robie	Bridgetown, N.S.
	Pte.	Jackson, Roy Kenneth	Bridgetown, N.S.
	Pte.	Jarvis, Aubrey	Weymouth Falls, N.S.
	Pte.	Jarvis, Hilton Sydney	Weymouth Falls, N.S.

Living in Southville, N.S. (1987)

* Pte.	Jarvis, Malcolm	Weymouth Falls, N.S.
Pte.	Jarvis, Ralph	Weymouth Falls, N.S.
Pte.	Johnson, Arthur	Newport Station, N.S.
Pte.	Johnson, Frank	Newport Station, N.S.
Corp.	Johnson, George Albert	Newport Station, N.S.
Pte.	Johnson, Stephen	Weymouth, N.S.
Pte.	Johnson, William	Newport Station, N.S.
Pte.	Jones, Glendower	Bridgetown, N.S.
Pte.	Jones, William Alfred	Liverpool, N.S.
Pte.	Lindsay, Frederick Leroy	Kentville, N.S.
Pte.	Lucaw, Thomas Grandy	Annapolis Royal, N.S.
Pte.	Marsman, Ezekial	Middleton, N.S.
Pte.	Middleton, Frank Edward	Weymouth Falls, N.S.
Pte.	Middleton, Ralph	Weymouth Falls, N.S.
Pte.	Owens, Charles Alfred	Bridgetown, N.S.
Pte.	Owens, Norman	Bridgetown, N.S.
Pte.	Pannill, Chester	Yarmouth, N.S.
Pte.	Paris, Garfield	Newport Station, N.S.
Pte.	Parker, Laurie	Granville Ferry, N.S.
Pte.	Parker, William Richmond	Kentville, N.S.
Pte.	Pleasant, Wallace James	Weymouth Falls, N.S.
Pte.	Ruggles, Harry	Annapolis Royal, N.S.
Pte.	Simmons, Aubrey	Weymouth Falls, N.S.
Pte.	Simmons, Harold	Kentville, N.S.
Pte.	Sims, Arthur	Bridgetown, N.S.
Sgt.	Smith, Charles Nathan M.	Yarmouth, N.S.
** Pte.	Smith, John	Newport Station, N.S.
Pte.	Smith, Reuben Alexander	Weymouth Falls, N.S.
Pte.	States, Cornelius	Mapleton, N.S.
Pte.	States, Harold	Mapleton, N.S.
Pte.	Stephenson, Ernest Alonza	Granville Ferry, N.S.
Pte.	Stephenson, Hallet Frederick	Digby, N.S.
Pte.	Stevens, John William	Yarmouth, N.S.
Pte.	Stevens, Leslie Hiram	Yarmouth, N.S.
Pte.	Stevenson, Moses	Thorne's Cove, N.S.
Pte.	Tyler, Fletcher	Bridgetown, N.S.
Pte.	Wesley, Benjamin	Greenville, N.S.
Pte.	Wesley, William	New Edinburgh, N.S.
Pte.	Williams, Samuel Austin	Shelburne, N.S.
Pte.	Wilson, Austin	Greenville, N.S.
Pte.	Wilson, Harry Nathaniel	Shelburne, N.S.
Pte.	Wilson, James Arlington	Yarmouth, N.S.
Pte.	Young, Stanley Charles	Liverpool, N.S.

Halifax-Dartmouth

Capt.	Livingston, Roderick	Dartmouth, N.S.
Lieut.	Haynes, James Bertram	Halifax, N.S.
Pte.	Allison, Walter Roland	Hammonds Plains, N.S.
Pte.	Anderson, Mackerrow	Hammonds Plains, N.S.
Pte.	Bauld, Frederick	Dartmouth, N.S.
Pte.	Blue, John	Dartmouth, N.S.
Pte.	Bonnett, Fred	Halifax, N.S.
Pte.	Brown, Samuel	Halifax, N.S.
Pte.	Brown, William George	Dartmouth, N.S.
Pte.	Bundy, Henry William	Cherry Brook, N.S.
Pte.	Bundy, William Henry	Cherry Brook, N.S.
Pte.	Butler, George Horace	Halifax, N.S.
Pte.	Byers, Andrew	Halifax, N.S.

Living in Cambridge, Mass. (1987)
**Living in Middleton, N.S. (1987)*

APPENDIX A

* Pte.	Carter, William	Halifax, N.S.
Pte.	Cartier, Charles	Halifax, N.S.
Pte.	Carvery, Vincent	Halifax, N.S.
Pte.	Cassidy, Robert	Halifax, N.S.
Pte.	Collins, Samuel	Halifax, N.S.
Pte.	David, Bernard	Dartmouth, N.S.
Pte.	David, Sydney	Halifax, N.S.
Pte.	Davidson, Wilfred Jones	Halifax, N.S.
Sgt.-Maj.	DeCosta, Wilfred A.	Halifax, N.S.
Pte.	Diggs, George Henry J.	Halifax, N.S.
Pte.	Dixon, Wallace	Halifax, N.S.
Pte.	Downey, George	Halifax, N.S.
Pte.	Downey, James	Halifax, N.S.
Pte.	Drummond, Charles	Preston Road, N.S.
Pte.	Fletcher, Ralph	Halifax, N.S.
Pte.	Flint, Stanley	Halifax, N.S.
Pte.	Franklin, Peter	Halifax, N.S.
Pte.	Fraser, James	Halifax, N.S.
Pte.	Goffigan, Thomas	Hammonds Plains, N.S.
Pte.	Grant, John Henry	Dartmouth, N.S.
Pte.	Grosse, Ernest Andrew	Dartmouth, N.S.
Pte.	Grosse, James	Beechville, N.S.
Pte.	Grosse, William	Beechville, N.S.
Pte.	Hamilton, Charles	Beechville, N.S.
Pte.	Harrison, George Washington	Halifax, N.S.
Pte.	Jackson, Charles William	Halifax, N.S.
Pte.	James, Robert Henry	Halifax, N.S.
Sgt.	Johnson, Walter Adolphus	Halifax, N.S.
Pte.	Jones, William	Hammonds Plains, N.S.
Pte.	Kellum, Edward	Halifax, N.S.
Corp.	Kellum, William	Halifax, N.S.
Pte.	Lambert, Harold	Halifax, N.S.
Pte.	Lambert, John	Halifax, N.S.
Pte.	Lattimore, Gilbert Richard	Halifax-Dartmouth, N.S.
Pte.	Lee, Cecil Roy	Halifax, N.S.
Pte.	Lee, Nathaniel	Fall River, N.S.
Pte.	Mansfield, John	Dartmouth, N.S.
Pte.	Mantley, Henry	Hammonds Plains, N.S.
Pte.	Mapp, Joseph	Halifax, N.S.
Pte.	Middleton, Louis	Dartmouth, N.S.
Pte.	Mitchell, Aubrey	Halifax, N.S.
Pte.	Mitchell, Harry	Hammonds Plains, N.S.
Sgt.-Maj.	Norman, James Phillip	Halifax, N.S.
Pte.	Parris, James	Halifax, N.S.
Pte.	Richardson, William	Halifax, N.S.
Pte.	Roachford, Walton Lindsay	Halifax, N.S.
Pte.	Ross, Charles	Halifax, N.S.
Pte.	Ross, Stephen	Halifax, N.S.
Pte.	Samuels, Wilford Martin	Halifax, N.S.
Sgt.	Sealy, Edward	Halifax, N.S.
Pte.	Skinner, Adolphus Francis	Halifax, N.S.
Pte.	Some, Charlie	Halifax, N.S.
Pte.	Steward, David Alfred	Halifax, N.S.
Pte.	Steward, Nathaniel	Halifax, N.S.
Pte.	Symonds, Richard Stanley	Upper Hammonds Plains, N.S.
Pte.	Tabb, Harold Coleman	Halifax, N.S.
Sgt.	Thomas, William Joseph	Halifax, N.S.

Living in Halifax, N.S. (1987)

	Pte.	Thompson, Charles	Halifax, N.S.
	Pte.	Tolliver, George Washington	Halifax, N.S.
	Pte.	Tolliver, William	Halifax, N.S.
	Pte.	Turner, Benjamin Paris	Halifax, N.S.
	Pte.	Turner, Harry	Halifax, N.S.
	Pte.	Turner, Samuel	Halifax, N.S.
	Pte.	Tynes, Archie	Dartmouth, N.S.
	Pte.	Tynes, Byron Hatfield	Dartmouth, N.S.
	Pte.	Tynes, James Frederick	Dartmouth, N.S.
	Pte.	Tynes, Reggie	Halifax, N.S.
	Pte.	Welch, James Edward	Dartmouth, N.S.
	Pte.	Williams, John	Preston, N.S.
	Pte.	Williams, Roy	Halifax, N.S.
	Pte.	Wilson, Gordon Charles	Upper Hammonds Plains, N.S.
	Pte.	Wilson, William	Halifax, N.S.
	Sgt.	Young, John James	Halifax, N.S.
New Brunswick	Lieut.	MacLean, Russell Roderick R.	Moncton, N.B.
	Pte.	Albert, George Randolph	Saint John, N.B.
	Pte.	Austin, Louis	Saint John, N.B.
	Pte.	Blizzard, John Spencer	Saint John, N.B.
	Pte.	Bushfan, Ernest Garfield	Saint John, N.B.
	Pte.	Bushfan, Harold Frederick	Saint John, N.B.
	Pte.	Bushfan, Phillip Andrew	Saint John, N.B.
	Pte.	Bushfan, Robert James	Saint John, N.B.
	Pte.	Carty, Albert	Saint John, N.B.
	Pte.	Claybourne, Frank Morris	Barker's Point, N.B.
	Sgt.	Coates, Duckworth	Frederick, N.B.
	Pte.	Dixon, Fred Charles	Saint John, N.B.
	Pte.	Dixon, George Richard	Saint John, N.B.
	Pte.	Eatman, John Wesley	Fredericton, N.B.
	Pte.	Hayes, Roy Edward	Saint John, N.B.
	Pte.	Hayes, Walter Roy	Saint John, N.B.
	Pte.	Holmes, James	Saint John, N.B.
	Pte.	Jones, Harry Timothy	Saint John, N.B.
	Pte.	Kennedy, Fred	Saint John, N.B.
	Pte.	Lupee, Frederick Oral	Saint John, N.B.
	Pte.	McCarthy, Harold	Saint John, N.B.
	Pte.	McIntyre, Charles Theodore	Saint John, N.B.
	Pte.	Martin, Joseph Edward	Westmorland Point, N.B.
	Pte.	Nichols, Herbert	Saint John, N.B.
	Pte.	O'Ree, Charles William	Fredericton, N.B.
	* Pte.	Richards, Percy James	Saint John, N.B.
	Pte.	Sadlier, James Albert	Saint John, N.B.
	Pte.	Simpson, Charles	Saint John, N.B.
	Sgt.	Stewart, George William	Saint John, N.B.
	Pte.	Thomas, Percy William	Saint John, N.B.
	Pte.	Tyler, Arthur Seymour	Saint John, N.B.
	Pte.	Tyler, Charles Elijah	Saint John, N.B.
	Pte.	Washington, Edward Syeth	Fredericton, N.B.
Western Canada	Capt.	Gayfer, Arthur John	Edmonton, Alta.
	Capt.	Young, William Lee	Calgary, Alta.
	Pte.	Alexander, Roy	Victoria, B.C.
	Pte.	Boon, William	Junkins, Alta.
	Pte.	Bowen, Columbus	Paxson, Alta.
	Pte.	Brooks, George Semperius	Winnipeg, Man.
	Pte.	Butler, Joseph Roger	Calgary, Alta.

*Living in Saint John, N.B. (1987)

	Corp.	Greenidge, Hewburn Nathaniel	Winnipeg, Man.
	Pte.	Harris, Arnold William	Revelstoke, B.C.
	Pte.	House, William	Edmonton, Alta.
*	Pte.	Jamerson, Robert	Athabasca Landing, Alta.
	Pte.	Lindsay, John	Junkins, Alta.
	Pte.	Marshall, James Henry	Calgary, Alta.
	Pte.	Virgil, Damascus	Edmonton, Alta.
	Pte.	Walton, Charles	Athabasca Landing, Alta.
	Pte.	Ware, Arthur Nelson	Calgary, Alta.
	Pte.	Ware, William James	Calgary, Alta.
	Pte.	West, Quester	Athabasca Landing, Alta.
	Pte.	Whims, James Douglas	Saltspring Island, B.C.
	Pte.	Whims, Robert Clark	Saltspring Island, B.C.
	Pte.	Williams, William	Athabasca Landing, B.C.
	Pte.	Wintworth, James Edward	Saltspring Island, B.C.

Ontario

	Capt.	Grant, James Stewart	Ottawa, Ont.
	Capt.	Morrison, Kenneth Allan	Ottawa, Ont.
	Lieut.	Fyles, Ernest N. Halton	Ottawa, Ont.
	Lieut.	Machean, Gillan Christie	Ottawa, Ont.
	Lieut.	Young, Leslie Bruce	Hamilton, Ont.
	Pte.	Alexander, Louis	Windsor, Ont.
	Pte.	Bell, Ernest Alexander	Hamilton, Ont.
**	Corp.	Binga, Bethune D.	Chatham, Ont.
	Pte.	Blencowe, Frank	Chatham, Ont.
	Pte.	Bowsell, Nathaniel S.	Chatham, Ont.
	Pte.	Bright, Arthur	St. Catharines, Ont.
	Pte.	Bright, Norman	St. Catharines, Ont.
	Pte.	Brown, Andrew	Brantford, Ont.
	Pte.	Bryant, Charles Henry	Hamilton, Ont.
	Pte.	Butler, John Everett	Lucan, Ont.
	Pte.	Cook, William	Toronto, Ont.
	Corp.	Courtney, Henry Francis	Guelph, Ont.
	Pte.	Crosby, Herbert Henderson	Chatham, Ont.
	Pte.	Day, Harry Linden	Toronto, Ont.
	Pte.	Dolman, Ambrose	Chatham, Ont.
	Pte.	Dorsey, Joseph Mellivan	St. Catharines, Ont.
	Corp.	Duncan, Frank H.	Cayuga, Ont.
	Pte.	Ellis, Edward D.	Chatham, Ont.
	Pte.	Ellsworth, Leo	Dresden, Ont.
	Pte.	Gaines, Gordon	Guelph, Ont.
	Pte.	Gaines, Victor	Guelph, Ont.
	Pte.	Goodwin, James	Dresden, Ont.
	Pte.	Goodwin, John	Dresden, Ont.
	Pte.	Grant, John Shadall	St. Catharines, Ont.
	Pte.	Harris, Jacob Henry	Windsor, Ont.
	Pte.	Hedgeman, George Henry	Swansea, Ont.
	Pte.	Henderson, James	Ingersoll, Ont.
	Pte.	Henderson, Richard Phillip	Chatham, Ont.
	Pte.	Higdon, William Rex	Dresden, Ont.
	Pte.	Johnson, James	Dresden, Ont.
	Pte.	Johnson, Joseph	Dresden, Ont.
	Pte.	Johnson, Noah	Dresden, Ont.
	Pte.	Jones, Thomas Harold	Windsor, Ont.
	Pte.	Jones, Thomas Jefferson	Beaverton, Ont.
	Pte.	Kelly, Charles	Ingersoll, Ont.
	Pte.	Lane, John James	St. Catharines, Ont.

Living in Winnipeg, Man. (1987)
**Living in Leamington, Ont. (1985)*

Pte.	Lewis, Frederick	Hamilton, Ont.
Pte.	Lewis, Walter Albert	Chatham, Ont.
Pte.	Lockman, James Woodson W.	Windsor, Ont.
Pte.	Lockman, Jerome Wellington	Windsor, Ont.
Pte.	Logan, Harry Alexander	London, Ont.
Pte.	Lucas, Walter James	Dresden, Ont.
Pte.	Lynch, Roy Ernest	Belleville, Ont.
Pte.	Madden, Joseph Alfred	St. Catharines, Ont.
Pte.	Matthews, Matthew George	Sandwich, Ont.
Pte.	Miller, Joshua	Hamilton, Ont.
Pte.	Miller, Russell	London, Ont.
Pte.	Morris, John William	Chatham, Ont.
Pte.	Moxley, Andrew Melvin	London, Ont.
Pte.	Nelson, Charles	Toronto, Ont.
Pte.	Patterson, Frederick	Windsor, Ont.
Pte.	Phoenix, Clifford	London, Ont.
Pte.	Robinson, William	Billings Bridge, Ont.
Pte.	Samson, Daniel	Beachville, Ont.
Pte.	Shreve, George Bolivar	North Buxton, Ont.
Pte.	Smith, William	Collingwood, Ont.
Pte.	Sullivan, John	Toronto, Ont.
Pte.	Sullivan, John Lewis	Toronto, Ont.
Pte.	Thomas, Robert Sumner	Windsor, Ont.
Pte.	Thornton, Samuel	Hamilton, Ont.
Pte.	Vandyke, Clarence	Dresden, Ont.
Pte.	Wales, James Huston	Dresden, Ont.
Pte.	Ward, Ray	Chatham, Ont.
Pte.	White, George	Windsor, Ont.
Pte.	Williams, John Charles	St. Catharines, Ont.
Pte.	Wimbish, George	Hamilton, Ont.
Pte.	Wright, Cornelius	Chatham, Ont.

Quebec

Pte.	Bradshaw, Ernest	Montreal, Que.
Pte.	Gale, William	Montreal, Que.
Pte.	Greenidge, Daniel	Montreal, Que.
Pte.	Jones, Henry Morgan	Montreal, Que.
Corp.	Livingstone, Daniel	Montreal, Que.
Pte.	Taylor, William Isaac	Montreal, Que.

U.S.A.

Pte.	Allen, Fessie	Helena, Mont.
Pte.	Allen, James	Birmingham, Ala.
Pte.	Austin, Cyrus	New Haven, Conn.
Pte.	Baker, John	Atlanta, Ga.
Pte.	Banks, Ernest	Connellsville, Pa.
Pte.	Barnes, Benjamin	Macon, Ga.
Pte.	Battle, Charles	Richmond, Mo.
Pte.	Bennett, George	Alexandria, La.
Pte.	Bennette, William	Birmingham, Ala.
Pte.	Black, William	Ewaric, N.J.
Pte.	Bland, Ellis	Bloomington, Ill.
Pte.	Brent, Robert	Baltimore, Md.
Pte.	Briscoe, George	Denver, Col.
Pte.	Brooks, Cornelius J.	Macon, Ga.
Pte.	Brown, Charles E.	Baltimore, Md.
Pte.	Bush, Leon	Chicago, Ill.
Pte.	Carr, Gaile	Clarksville, Tenn.
Pte.	Castor, Lewis L.	Buffalo, N.Y.
Pte.	Clark, Ellwood	Lexington, N.Y.
Pte.	Cobby, Thomas	Cincinnati, Oh.
Pte.	Cooper, Early	Darlington, S.C.

Pte.	Crogger, William E.	Indianapolis, Ind.
Pte.	Dabney, Percy	Detroit, Mich.
Pte.	Darden, James	Arlington, Va.
Pte.	Davis, Fred	Columbus, Oh.
Pte.	Davis, Fred A.	Columbus, Oh.
Pte.	Davis, Phillip	Little Rock, Ark.
Pte.	Davis, Roy	Morgantown, W.Va.
Pte.	Deerhart, William	Knoxville, Tenn.
Pte.	Devon, Walter	Pensacola, Fla.
Pte.	Dorris, Alfred	Kansas City, Mo.
Pte.	Dorsey, Lun	Virginia, Ind.
Pte.	Douglas, William Hamilton	New Orleans, La.
Pte.	Eatman, Manzer	Washington, D.C.
Pte.	Falawn, Marlow	Lowell, Mass.
Pte.	Foster, Mitchell	Oklahoma City, Okla.
Pte.	Francis, Shirley	Ethridge, Tenn.
Pte.	Freeman, Ralph S.	Springfield, Mass.
Pte.	Gains, John Lonza	Memphis, Tenn.
Pte.	Gans, Young Joe	Grand Forks, N.Dak.
Pte.	Garey, William D.	Macon, Ga.
Pte.	Garnett, Wallace	Birmingham, Ala.
Pte.	Garth, Robert	Louisville, Ky.
Pte.	Gates, Harry	Seyrene, Ala.
Pte.	Guerry, Elmo	U.S.A.
Pte.	Hall, Edward	Cleveland, Oh.
Pte.	Hamilton, Stanley	Moysville, Ky.
Pte.	Harall, George	Paducak, Ky.
Pte.	Harper, William LeRoy	Paola, Kan.
Pte.	Harris, Oscar	Logansport, Ind.
Pte.	Harris, William	New Orleans, La.
Sgt.	Hemphill, Curry Carter	Atlanta, Ga.
Pte.	Henderson, Donald	Detroit, Mich.
Pte.	Hill, Ramon	Maplesville, Ala.
Pte.	Hogue, William	Boston, Mass.
Pte.	Hollie, Clinton	Oxford, Miss.
Pte.	Holloway, Edward Rice	Newport, R.I.
Pte.	Holloway, Ulysses	Charleston, S.C.
Pte.	Hunt, William	Raleigh, N.C.
Pte.	Hunter, Harry	Gainsville, Ga.
Pte.	Hyde, James	Detroit, Mich.
Pte.	Jackson, Milton	Knoxville, Tenn.
Pte.	Jenifer, Lemuel	Detroit, Mich.
Pte.	Johnson, Melvan	Jasper, Mich.
Pte.	Johnson, Obediah	Jackson, Ga.
Pte.	Johnson, Walter	New Orleans, La.
Pte.	Jones, Charles Manuel	South Bend, Ind.
Pte.	Jones, Meadows	Detroit, Mich.
Pte.	Jones, Paul	Mill Brook, N.C.
Pte.	Kelly, Frank S.	U.S.A.
Pte.	Kelly, George	Kalamazoo, Mich.
Pte.	Kirksey, Milton	Bessemer, Ala.
Pte.	Lewis, John Madison	Orange, N.J.
Pte.	Lockwood, Robert	Sewickley, Pa.
Pte.	McArthur, Chester	Detroit, Mich.
Pte.	McDowell, Claud	Forest City, N.C.
Pte.	McNeil, Clemens	Shreveport, La.
Pte.	Macon, Ivan	Chicago, Ill.
Pte.	Madison, Edward	Delaware, Oh.
Pte.	Marsh, Harry Boyd	Newark, N.J.
Pte.	Martin, Buster	Hot Springs, Ark.

Pte.	Massey, Luther Levi	Amherst, Va.
Corp.	Miles, Harry	Pittsburgh, Pa.
Pte.	Miner, Melvan	Ypsilanti, Mich.
Pte.	Mitchell, John	Ypsilanti, Mich.
Pte.	Mitchell, Vergil	Chicago, Ill.
Pte.	Mitchell, William Eugene	Franklinton, N.C.
Pte.	Monroe, John	Memphis, Tenn.
Pte.	Moore, Horace	Rockingham, N.C.
Pte.	Moore, Walter	Norfolk, Va.
Pte.	Nealy, Loris	Chicago, Ill.
Pte.	Nichols, Roscoe	Higginsville, Mo.
Pte.	Overton, John Stephenson	New Albany, Ind.
Pte.	Parker, Anthony	Sacramento, Cal.
Sgt.	Patterson, John Leonard	Battle Creek, Mich.
Pte.	Payne, Charles	Orange, Va.
Pte.	Perkins, Anderson Edward	Nashville, Tenn.
Pte.	Pettiford, Jesse Finck	Detroit, Mich.
Pte.	Phillips, Charles	Little Rock, Ark.
Pte.	Phillips, Henry	Dodgeburg, Tenn.
Pte.	Pierce, John Wesley	Cambridge, Mass.
Pte.	Platt, Abe	U.S.A.
Pte.	Prather, Gus	U.S.A.
Pte.	Redmond, Daniel	U.S.A.
Pte.	Reid, John Walter	Plateau, Ala.
Pte.	Robinson, Charles	U.S.A.
Pte.	Robinson, Louis Woodward	Chicago, Ill.
Pte.	Robinson, William	Montgomery, Ala.
Pte.	Rodgers, William	Detroit, Mich.
Pte.	St. Claire, Earle	Manhattan, N.Y.
Pte.	Sallee, Clarence	Springfield, Ill.
Pte.	Sargeant, Samuel	Philadelphia, Pa.
Pte.	Savage, William	Portsmouth, Vt.
Pte.	Scott, George	Detroit, Mich.
Pte.	Simmonds, James	Atlanta, Ga.
Pte.	Smith, Arthur	Jacksonville, Fla.
Pte.	Smith, Lafayette	Chicago, Ill.
Pte.	Smith, Narvaeg	Columbus, Oh.
Pte.	Smith, Samuel	Norfolk, Va.
Pte.	Smith, Willie	Columbia, S.C.
Pte.	Stephen, David	Flatwood, Ala.
Pte.	Steward, Percy	Stanford, Ky.
Pte.	Stewart, James	Savannah, Ga.
Pte.	Stone, Joseph	Dyersburg, Tenn.
Pte.	Sumlar, James	Ypsilanti, Mich.
Pte.	Syttles, Harry	Atlanta, Ga.
Pte.	Taylor, Arthur	Lafayette, La.
Pte.	Taylor, William	Yozoo, Miss.
Pte.	Thomas, William	Birmingham, Ala.
Pte.	Tivis, John Bennett	Richmond, Ky.
Pte.	Tolbert, James Arthur	Detroit, Mich.
Pte.	Toulmin, Alexander	Mobile, Ala.
Pte.	Trice, Ben	Pembroke, Ky.
Pte.	Tudor, Alfred Augustus	New Albany, Ind.
Pte.	Turner, Will	Memphis, Tenn.
Pte.	Wallace, Samuel E.	Charleston, W.Va.
Pte.	Walton, Archer	Louisville, Ky.
Pte.	Ward, Joseph	Farmville, N.C.
Pte.	Watson, James	Harlers, Miss.
Pte.	Webster, Harrison	Fergus Falls, Minn.
Pte.	Welford, John	Morristown, Pa.

Pte.	Whitaker, John	U.S.A.
Pte.	White, Jesse	Atlanta, Ga.
Pte.	Wigfall, Jesse	Edgeton, N.C.
Pte.	Williams, Coleman	Ferriday, La.
Pte.	Williams, Edward	St. Charles, Mo.
Pte.	Williams, Eugene	Atlanta, Ga.
Pte.	Williams, Frank	Atlanta, Ga.
Pte.	Williams, Henry	Shaw, Miss.
Pte.	Williams, John	South Omaha, Neb.
Pte.	Williams, Samuel Austin	Harveysburg, Oh.
Pte.	Williams, Tillman McKinley	Smithville, Tenn.
Pte.	Willis, John	U.S.A.
Pte.	Wilson, Harvey	Detroit, Mich.
Pte.	Wilson, Ottinger	U.S.A.
Pte.	Woodson, John	Louisburg, N.C.
Pte.	Wright, Henry	U.S.A.
Pte.	Wright, James Hillier	Denver, Col.
Pte.	Young, John	Houston, Tex.
Pte.	Young, Nathaniel	East St. Louis, Ill.
Pte.	Young, William	Braggs, Ala.
Pte.	Youngstein, Charley	Newburgh, N.Y.
Pte.	Zeigber, Rubin	New Rochelle, N.Y.

106th Battalion, CEF

Pte.	Anstey, William	Halifax, N.S.
Pte.	Ash, Norman	Antigonish, N.S.
Pte.	Ash, Rollie	Antigonish, N.S.
Pte.	Bowles, Morley	Amherst, N.S.
Pte.	Clyke, James Arthur	Truro, N.S.
Corp.	Gaskin, Hugh Allan	Sydney, N.S.
Corp.	Halfkenny, Clinton	Amherst, N.S.
Corp.	Halfkenny, Herbert	Amherst, N.S.
Pte.	Johnson, Gordon	Truro, N.S.
Pte.	Jones, Irving Thomas	Truro, N.S.
Pte.	Jones, Jeremiah	Truro, N.S.
* Pte.	Jones, Sydney Morgan	Truro, N.S.
Pte.	Martin, Percy	Amherst, N.S.
Pte.	Roach, Nathaniel	Sydney, N.S.
Pte.	Stoutley, Ralph Leslie	Guysborough, N.S.
Pte.	Taylor, Frank	Sydney, N.S.

Living in Halifax, N.S. (1987)

The names were taken from the nominal rolls of the No. 2 and 106th battalions. This is not intended as a comprehensive listing of all the Black veterans who served in World War I. I express my regrets at the inadvertent omission of any names or information.

APPENDIX B

Minister of Militia & Defence
Ottawa.

Nov 6/1914

Dear Sir :—

The colored people of Canada want to know why they are not allowed to enlist in the Canadian militia. I am informed that several who have applied for enlistment in the Canadian expeditionary forces have been refused for no other apparent reason than their color, as they were physically and mentally fit.

Thanking you in advance for any information that you can & will give me in regards to this matter I remain yours Respectfully, for King & Country.

Arthur Alexander
North Buxton, Ont.

R.Q. 297-1-21.   I.

Nov. 20th, 1914.

Sir,-

The Honorable Minister of Militia and
Defence has duly received your letter of 6th instant
enquiring about coloured people not being allowed
to enlist in the Canadian Militia for Overseas
Expeditionary Force.

Under instructions already issued, the
selection of Officers and men for the second contingent
is entirely in the hands of Commanding Officers, and
their selections or rejections are not interfered with
from Headquarters.

I have the honour to be,
Sir,
Your obedient servant,

Lt.-Col.
Military Secretary.

Arthur Alexander, Esq.,
North Buxton,
Ont.

Original in Public Archives of Canada, Ottawa

Canadian Pacific Railway Company's Telegraph

T. B. Form 18

TERMS AND CONDITIONS

All messages are received by this Company for transmission, subject to the terms and conditions printed on their Blank Form No. 2, which terms and conditions have been agreed to by the sender of the following message. This is an unrepeated message, and is delivered by request of the sender under these conditions.

W. J.CAMP, Assistant Manager, Montreal, Que.   W.MARSHALL, Assistant Manager, Winnipeg, Man.
D. H. BOWEN, Supt., Sudbury, Ont.   R. N. YOUNG, Supt., Vancouver, B. C.
H. J. LILLIE, Supt., Toronto, Ont.   D. L. HOWARD, Supt., Calgary, Alta.   **J. McMILLAN,**
A. C. FRASER, Supt., Montreal, Que.   D. COONS, Supt., Moose Jaw, Sask.
W. M. GODSOE, Supt., St. John, N. B.   R. M. PAYNE, Supt., Winnipeg, Man.   Manager Telegraphs, Montreal.

b9ra y 27-2 Extra

StJohn NB Nov 18th-15

Secretary Militia Council

Ottawa Ont.

Is there a colored Battalion being formed in any part

of Canada twenty colored men here have passed medical examination

and are anxious to go.

                    Beverley R Armstrong

3pm   Lt Col.

Sir Sam Hughes, M.P.
Ottawa, Ontario
CANADA
Nov. 21, 1915

Hon. Sir:

On behalf of St. John's Colored residents I desire to return thanks to you for remarks made in regards to Colored Men enlisting in Canada's fighting lines. I received a letter from you along the same lines, dated October 6/15. I showed the letter to the Colored Boys shortly after it reached me. Some of them tried to enlist but were turned down. I sent them back again with the threat that I would call for a showdown if they did not get a chance, after a while 20 were accepted, sworn in, etc., ordered to be ready to join the 104th at Sussex, 15 Nov. They reported, went forward at noon with about 50 Whites.

On arrival they met the 2nd Commanding Officer who told them he knew nothing of their coming, and to get right away from there as he would not have them at all, in fact insulted them. He told them that a Colored Battalion was being formed in Ontario and to go there. They arrived back in the city at 9:30, the same night Nov. 15/15. Reported to the recruiting office Mill St., they were told there to come around in the morning. They went from there to other Recruiting Officers, but nothing has been done for them.

They have been told that they are not on the payroll, not entitled to sub-sistence money, and that in fact they are only Militia men. These men are all poor men, some with families. On an average each was making at least $12.00 per week when they threw up their jobs to enlist and fight for their Empire and King.

Nothing has been done for these people by the Military here, it is a downright shame and an insult to the Race, the way our people has been used in regards to wanting to enlist, etc.

England and some of her allies are using many Colored troops, and the Colored people are talking of appealing to the embassys at Washington whose countries are using Colored Men to be allowed to enter the Foreign services.

I have counseled against this as I believe you will right the wrong.

I wish you would have this matter cleared up at your earliest moment of leisure and issue a general order that Colored, where fit, shall not be discriminated against by the Military Recruiting Officers in Canada.

I am quite against a Battalion myself as I am directly opposed to segregation.

Yours "for a square deal for each and for all"

[Sgd.] John T. Richards
274 Prince William St.

P.S. Enclosing news comments from leading papers, Nov. 20.

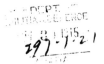

c

Nov. 25th, 1915.

Private.

Dear Sir,-

I am in receipt of your letter of the
21st instant, in behalf of St. John's colored residents,
who are desirous of enlisting for Overseas service.
I have given instructions that colored
men are to be permitted to enlist in any battalion, and I
shall be pleased to hand your letter over to my Adjutant
General for immediate report in connection with the
circumstances mentioned by you. As soon as I get a
report I will write you again.

Faithfully,

(sgd) SAM HUGHES

John T. Richards, Esq.,
    274 Princetown St.,
        St. John, N.B.

I.T.

DEPT.
MILITIA DEFENCE
FEB 31 1915
292-1-21
CANADA

29th November,1915.

From -
      The Adjutant-General,
      Canadian Militia.

To -
      The G.O.C.6th Division,
      Halifax,N.S.

Re enlistment of
coloured men in
Canadian Forces.

Sir,

I have the honour,by direction,to enclose herewith,copy of a letter from Mr. John T.Richards,St.John,
N.B.,addressed to the Honourable the Minister,regarding
enlistment of coloured men in the Canadian Forces.

2.   It is the desire of the Honourable the Minister
that you should have this matter investigated immediately,
forwarding a full report to Militia Headquarters on the
matter of the enlistment of the men referred to, and the
refusal of the O.C.104th Battalion to accept these men
after having been sent forward by the recruiting officer.
A great many complaints have been received from coloured
men in regard to their treatment and the Honourable the
Minister has given instructions that the coloured men
are to be permitted to enlist in any battalion.

3.   As this matter is urgent you are requested to
make immediate investigation and report.

           I have the honour to be,
               Sir,
           Your obedient Servant,

                                3)

Original in Public Archives of Canada, Ottawa
                         Brigadier-General,
                    Actg.Adjutant-General.

PEC

M. F. B. 239.
300M—8-15.
H.Q. 1772-39-194.

In any further correspondence on this subject please quote Number and Date of this Communication.

No. 11 M.D. 99-4-7.

297-1-21

Victoria, B.C. December, 9th, 1915

From The D.O.C. M.D. No. 11.

Victoria, B.C.

To The Secretary, Militia Council,

Headquarters, OTTAWA.

ENLISTMENT
Coloured Recruits.

Sir,

I have the honour to forward herewith copies of letters received from Mr Henshaw, Recruiting Officer, and the Officer Commanding, 23rd, Infantry Brigade, Vancouver, B.C for Headquarters consideration.

2.   It is submitted that there being comparatively so small a number of negros and coloured persons in British Columbia, and the colour line being very sharply drawn as compared with Eastern Canada, it is most inadvisable that negros or coloured men should be enlisted into the same units as white men. Several cases of coloured applicants for enlistment have been reported on by Officers Commanding units and the universal opinion is that if this were allowed it would do much harm, as white men here will not serve in the same ranks with negros or coloured persons.

3.   It is therefore recommended that authority be granted to enlist negros and coloured men in a separate unit, and that they be sent forward as a draft to join similar units organized in the East.

I have the honour to be,
Sir,
Your obedient servant, -

Colonel,
D.O.C. M.D. No 11.

COPY

6.D.125-1-39.

Halifax,N.S. December 14th, 1915.

From:-
    The Officer Commanding,
        106th Overseas Battalion.
To:-
    The D.A.A. and Q.M.G.
        Sixth Division.

297-1-21

Re enlistmentof coloured men for overseas.

Sir,
    I have the honour to submit the following report on the marginally noted subject.
    Some time ago a man named Reese (coloured) of Truro,N.S., tried to enlist in Halifax either in the Composite or R.C.R. Captain Roscoe refused to take him unless he could bring a certain number of his fellow country men for service, at the same time referring him to me for enlistment in the 106th Battalion. After a recruiting meeting in Truro several weeks ago, a coloured minister - Rev.Mr.White approached me in regard to the matter, and I told him if he would get in touch with the coloured men throughout Nova Scotia, and raise enough for a platoon, I would take this platoon into my Regimant. He promised to get busy, but to date, I have only received about six names. Since that time, word has come from Ottawa that thefe is to be no distinction of colour for enlistments.
    As soon as this became known, several white men who had been about to sign on, refused to do so if coloured men wereto be admitted into the Regiment. Personally, I think coloured men should do their share in the Empire's Defence, and I believe that some of them would make good soldiers. Still, if I had my choice I would prefer white men, and if the enlistment of coloured men is going to prevent better men from signing on, it seems to me that the best thing to do would be to keep them separated. The proportion of coloured men wanting to enlist is very small, and I would feel very loath to risk the experiment of taking on negroes when plenty of white men were available. Neither my men nor myself, would care to sleep alongside them, or to eat with them, especially in warm weather. A white man's appetite is a peculiar thing.
    I trust that some solution may be found by which the services of coloured men may be utilized. In the meantime, I am not encouraging the enlistment of coloured men in the 106th Battalion, for reasons stated above.

                    I have the honour to be,
                        Sir,
                    Your obedient servant,

                (SIGNED) W.H.ALLEN, Lieut-Colonel,
            Commanding 106th "Overseas" Battalion.

Reprinted courtesy Public Archives of Canada, Ottawa

Rac...

Memorandum.   H.Q. 297-1-21.

DEPARTMENT OF MILITIA AND DEFENCE.

_To._

The Chief of the General Staff.   _Ottawa,_____ 21st March, 1916.

Formation of Coloured
Overseas Battalion.

At the present time, coloured men can be enlisted in an Overseas Battalion provided that the
Commanding Officer is willing to accept them.   The
question of the formation of a whole Battalion as a
Unit is raised in definite form by two letters just
received from D.O.C. M.D. No. 13, from which it would
appear that the Rev. C.W. Washington, who is described
as Archbishop of St. Mark's Church, Edmonton, is satis-
fied that a full Battalion can be raised - Officers
excepted.

I should be glad to have your views on this
subject.

My own view is that a Coloured Overseas Battalion
would not be of assistance to us at the present time,
as they could not be used as drafts.

[signature]

Major General.
A/Adjutant-General.

MEMORANDUM on the
----
enlistment of negroes in

Canadian Expeditionary Force.
----

    1.   Nothing is to be gained by blinking facts. The civilized negro is vain and imitative; in Canada he is not being impelled to enlist by a high sense of duty; in the trenches he is not likely to make a good fighter; and the average white man will not associate with him on terms of equality. Not a single commanding officer in Military District No. 2 is willing to accept a coloured platoon as part of his battalion (H.Q.297-1-29); and it would be humiliating to the coloured men themselves to serve in a battalion where they were not wanted.

    2.   In France, in the firing line, there is no place for a black battalion, C.E.F. It would be eyed askance; it would crowd out a white battalion; and it would be difficult to re-inforce.

    3.   Nor could it be left in England and used as a draft-giving depot; for there would be trouble if negroes were sent to the front for the purpose of reinforcing white battalions; and, if they are any good at all, they would resent being kept in Canada for the purpose of finding guards, &c.

    4.   It seems, therefore, that three courses are practicable:

        (a)   As at present, to allow negroes to enlist, individually, into white battalions at the discretion of commanding officers.

        (b)   To allow them to form one or more labour battalions. Negroes from Nova Scotia, for example, would not be unsuitable for the purpose.

        (c)   To ask the British Government if it can make use of a black battalion, C.E.F., on special duty overseas (e.g. in Egypt): but the battalion will not be ready before the fall, and, if only on account of its relatively extravagant rates of pay, it will not mix well with other troops.

    5.   I recommend courses (a) and (b).

P/ W.Gwatkin

                Major-General,
13.4.16.   Chief of the General Staff.

House of Commons Debates
March 24, 1916

Enlistment of Coloured Men

On the Orders of the Day:

Hon. WILLIAM PUGSLEY: Have any effective steps been taken to
enable coloured citizens of Canada who are desirous of enlisting for
service abroad to enlist, or for the formation of a regiment of coloured
citizens? I have brought this question before the House on at least
two previous occasions, in consequence of representations which were
made to me by some coloured citizens of New Brunswick, as well as
some from Ontario. The Minister of Militia made the statement that
the matter was under consideration. There is a good deal of complaint
and a very considerable amount of feeling among our coloured citizens
that they have not been treated fairly. They have been told that their
services would be accepted, and when they have gone to the recruiting
office where they were told to go, they have been sent away without
receiving any satisfaction. The Minister of Militia, I think, has in mind
the idea that a coloured regiment might be raised in Canada. I should
like to know what steps, if any, have been taken towards this end.

Hon. A. E. KEMP (Acting Minister of Militia and Defence): I understand there are a number of coloured people in the various units
throughout the country; but I am not aware that any effort has so far
been made to organize a unit composed wholly of coloured citizens.
Some steps may have been taken, but I have no information to that
effect at present. I shall make inquiries.

Reprinted courtesy Public Archives of Canada, Ottawa

August 29, 1917

Military Service Act

Military Service—The Military Service Act, 1917 (chapter 19), makes every British subject between the ages of twenty and forty-five, who is, or has been since August 4, 1914, resident in Canada, liable to be called out on active service, excepting clergy and persons exempted by the Act. Men who are liable to be called out are divided into six classes: (1) those between twenty and thirty-four who are unmarried or widowers with no child; (2) those of the same age who are married or widowers with a child; (3) those between thirty-five and forty who are unmarried or widowers with no child; (4) those of the same age who are married or widowers with a child; (5) those between forty and forty-five who are unmarried or widowers with no child; (6) those of the same age who are married or widowers with a child. A man who is liable to be called out may be exempted on the following grounds: that it is expedient he should continue his usual work, or be engaged in other non-military work, continue to be educated or trained; hardship arising from exceptional business obligations or domestic position; ill health or infirmity; conscientious objection on religious grounds. Claims of exemption are to be heard by local tribunals from which appeals may be made to provincial appeal tribunals and from these to a central appeal judge. Provisions are made in the Act for the appointment of these tribunals. Men are to be called out, by classes, by proclamation of the Governor-in-Council, and men so called out are to be deemed to be on leave of absence without pay until placed on active service. The Act authorizes the calling out of only one hundred thousand men. Penalties are imposed for contravention of or resistance to the Act.

Reprinted courtesy Public Archives of Canada, Ottawa

APPENDIX C

THE BLACK CULTURAL SOCIETY OF NOVA SCOTIA
PRESENTS A RECOGNITION BANQUET FOR

"VETERANS OF WORLD WAR ONE"
(1914-1918)

DATE: NOVEMBER 12, 1982
TIME: 7:30 P.M.
PLACE: LORD NELSON HOTEL
IMPERIAL BALLROOM, HALIFAX, N.S.

MUSICAL ENTERTAINMENT

DOOR PRIZES

ADMISSION:
$15.00 PER PERSON

November 10, 1982

Mr. Calvin W. Ruck, R. S. W.
Committee Co-Chairman
Black Cultural Society
27 Walker Street
Dartmouth, N.S.
B2X 1B2

Dear *Mr Ruck*

On the occasion of the Reunion and Recognition Dinner for Black Veterans, I wish to extend official congratulations on behalf of the City of Saint John.

It is a sad fact that we often forget those who paid the price for freedom on our behalf. Rudyard Kipling summed it up beautifully in his note, "It's Tommy this and Tommy that and chuck him out, the Brute - but its saviour of our country when the guns begin to shoot".

The Black Cultural Society deserves the thanks of all Canadians for the initiative and support they have shown in recognizing our Black Veterans.

To the surviving Veterans of the Number 2 Construction Battalion (Black) C.E.F, I extend the good wishes of all our citizens. May God grant them a long life and good health to enjoy it.

In conclusion, may I respectfully suggest that, through the medium of tape recordings, the memories of those distinguished Canadians be retained and that the Black Cultural Society, which has displayed so much leadership, initiate further research and publication of their role.

Again my sincere good wishes to all those who have supported the Reunion.

Sincerely yours,

A. R. W. Lockhart
Lieutenant-Colonel, CD
MAYOR

PRESIDENT   Ernest Jordan

SECRETARY   Anderson Gunn

17 September, 1982.

Mr. Calvin W. Ruck, R.S.W.
27 Walker St.
Dartmouth, N. S.
B2X 1B2

Dear Mr. Ruck:

We were interested in hearing about your project
for a re-union of members of No. 2 Construction Btn.
(Black) of World War I. Colonel Dan Sutherland, the
original C.O. of this Btn. was well known to the members
of this Branch. He continued to play an active part in
community affairs until his death a few years ago at the
age of 96.

Enclosed is a cheque for the sum of $50.00 as
a contribution towards the expenses of your planned
re-union. We wish you every success in the fulfillment
of your plans.

Sincerely yours,

PICTOU BRANCH, No. 16
ROYAL CANADIAN LEGION

Alastair E. Macdonald
Treasurer

Cambrai N.S. Branch No. 37
Royal Canadian Legion
MULGRAVE, NOVA SCOTIA
BOE 2GO

Box 62 Mulgrave N. S.
October 14th. 1982

Black Cultural Society
1016 Main Street
Dartmouth N. S.
B2W 4X9

Dear Sir;

Attached find a small donation towards your celebration, according to our records
that are available we had two Legion members in our area belonging to the 2nd.
construction Battalion. I will list them below for your information, I was very
well acquainted with both.

Connolly   George   Edward   No. 931243

Enlisted September 2nd. 1916   Age 16 yrs.

Discharged   February 15th. 1919

Served in Canada, England, France & Germany

Died March 26th. 1963 ------ Buried in St. Andrews Anglican cemetry
                                    Mulgrave N. S.

Parris   Joseph   Alexander   No. 931017

Enlisted July 25th. 1916   Age 17

Discharged February 10th. 1919

Served in Canada, England & France

Died April 19th. 1972 ------ Buried in St. Lawrence Catholic cemetry
                                    Mulgrave N. S.

Fraternally,

    E. K. Harding, Secretary.

BLACK CULTURAL SOCIETY OF NOVA SCOTIA

CERTIFICATE OF HONOUR

*AWARDED TO*_____

in recognition of service to
KING AND COUNTRY
DURING WORLD WAR ONE (1914 - 1918)

Presented at Reunion and Recognition Banquet
Halifax, N.S., November 12, 1982

APPENDIX D

Truro *Daily News*
August 17, 1917

A "D.C.M." for a Truro Soldier

Pte. Jerry Jones, Ford St., Runs in Bunch of Huns—Captures Their Machine Gun—Facetiously Hands M.G. Over to His C.O.

Has been recommended for Distinguished Conduct Medal—what a Truro Officer in England writes.

We believe the well-known, industrious and highly respected Truro colored man, Pte. Jerry Jones, a resident of Ford Street, who went overseas with the 106th Battalion, has scored a big hit in his scraps with the Huns at the front.

When Jerry Jones joined the 106th under Col. Innis, he was a strapping big fellow—a fine looking soldier—he took a humble position; played his part well; went overseas; volunteered for the battlefield and has been a terror to the treacherous German on more than one occasion.

He was lately wounded in action and is just recovering and nobly getting ready for his "bit" again.

He has shown himself a patriot, brave, powerful and resourceful, and we understand he has been recommended for the Distinguished Conduct Medal.

Here is a letter we have just received from a Truro officer in Witley Camp, England about some Truro heroes.

(Witley Camp, Surrey, July 25, 1917) All Nova Scotians, and especially those of us from Truro were delighted when we heard that Fred Huntley had won distinction for bravery at the front.

Word comes from those heroes, who are daily arriving in English hospitals of numerous acts of bravery on the part of our boys from home, many of which should be rewarded with V.C.'s, but will never reach beyond the eyes of those who are now past recording such events.

One of the humble citizens of Truro, always an honest, hard-working man was reported wounded several weeks ago. I last saw him in Bramshott in January before he had gone to France, had a few words with him, next heard he had been wounded and only today, from one of the lads in the hospital, who was with him at the time, did I hear the complete story of how "JERRY JONES" had captured a German machine gun, forced the crew to carry it back to our lines, and depositing it at the feet of the C.O. said: "Is this thing any good?" ("Isn't that just like our big, honest, witty Jerry?"—Ed. News.)

The report is that he has been recommended for a D.C.M. I hope it is true. All honor to this man, who is ready for the front again.

May he live to return to Truro and receive the welcome he deserves.

We are glad for those encouraging lines for the boys from a Military Camp in England and the thoughtful writer need never fear but what if "Jerry Jones" returns to Truro with a D.C.M. He'll be the lion of the hour.

We here can see that great big colored man, on the battlefield, without a word of German in his Ford Street vernacular order those cowardly Huns to pack up their machine gun and march to the British lines! Well done, Jerry.

Reprinted courtesy Truro Daily News

The Toronto Telegram
August 28, 1918

Colored Men Are Barred

Royal Air Force Restricts

Were Applicants Numerous Enough to Form a Company Their Enlistment Might Be Entertained.

That colored men are barred from the Royal Air Force in Canada is admitted by Capt. Seymour, of the Headquarters staff. "Were colored volunteers numerous enough to make up a company of their own, their applications might be entertained," he said, "but as they are few, it has been considered advisable to refuse all applications for enlistment."

The question was raised by the non-acceptance of Harold Leopold Bell, a Jamaican, 24 years of age, with wife and two children. He voluntarily enlisted in Boston, Mass., and was sent to Camp Sussex, N.B., last July. On August 21 he was given his discharge to come to Toronto to become a mechanic with the R.A.F. On his discharge paper he is described, "Complexion—Dark." He claims to be an expert machinist of seven years experience, and to know gas engines, yet when he reported to the recruiting depot at George and Duke streets with an inexperienced French-Canadian, the latter was accepted and he was rejected. NOT BOUND BY M.S.A.

Transportation back to Camp Sussex was offered him, but as he has been discharged from that unit, Bell has secured employment in a munition plant.

The Military Service Act drafts colored men, but the Royal Air Force does not come within the scope of the act. The R.A.F. are exercising the greatest care when applicants come from the States claiming they are British subjects, and now will not accept any evidence other than the birth certificate.

Reprinted courtesy Leo W. Bertley, author of Canada and Its People of African Descent

Ottawa,
October 28, 1916

Memorandum

Mr. Cory

I am just in receipt of a telegram from Mr. Malcolm N. J. Reid of Vancouver, which is badly transmitted but which indicates that an application has been made to him for the admission to Canada of coloured men from the United States to join a construction battalion.

Mr. Reid asks whether the Department will authorize the admission of coloured recruits for a construction battalion.

I think this should be turned down, judging from what I have seen and heard there is no great difficulty in securing recruits for forestry and construction battalions, and I think it would be unwise to allow a lot of coloured men to get a foothold in Canada, even under guise of enlistment in such a battalion.

W.D. Scott
Superintendent of Immigration

Reprinted courtesy Leo W. Bertley, author of Canada and Its People of African Descent

Black Soldier's Lament

By Captain George Borden
(to the tune of "The Green Beret")

The bugle called and forth we went
To serve the crown our backs far bent
And build what e're that must be done
But ne're to fire an angry gun
No heroes we not nay not one

With deep lament we did our job
Despite the shame our manhood robbed
We built and fixed and fixed again
To prove our worth as proud black men
And hasten sure the Kaiser's end

From Scotia port to Seaford Square
Across to France the conflict there
At Villa Lajoux and Place Péronne
For God and King to right the wrong
The number two six hundred strong

Stripped to the waist and sweated chest
Mid-day's reprieve much needed rest
We dug and hauled and lifted high
From trenches deep toward the sky
Non-fighting troops and yet we die

The peace restored the battle won
Black sweat and toil had beat the hun
Black blood was spilled black bodies maimed
For medals brave no black was named
Yet proud were we our pride unshamed

But time will bring forth other wars
Then give to us more daring chores
That we might prove our courage strong
Preserve the right repel the wrong
And proud we'll sing the battle song

COLORED MEN!

Your King and Country Need <u>YOU</u>!

<u>NOW</u> is the time to show your Patriotism and Loyalty.

WILL YOU HEED THE CALL AND DO YOUR SHARE?

□ □ □

Your Brothers of the Colonies have rallied to the Flag and are distinguishing themselves at the Front.

Here also is your opportunity to be identified in the Greatest War of History, where the Fate of Nations who stand for Liberty is at stake. Your fortunes are equally at stake as those of your White Brethren.

□ □ □

NO. 2 CONSTRUCTION BATTALION

Now being Organized All Over the Dominion Summons You. **WILL YOU SERVE?**

The British and their Allies are now engaged in a great forward movement. Roads, Bridges and Railways must be made to carry the Victors forward. The need of the day is Pioneers, Construction Companies and Railway Construction Companies. No. 1 Construction Company has been recruited. No. 2 Construction Company is now called for.

Lt. Col. D.H. Sutherland is in charge of the Company's Headquarters at Pictou; at Halifax applications may be made at the Parade Recruiting Station; elsewhere to any Recruiting Officer, or by letter to —

MAJOR W.B.A. RITCHIE, *Chief Recruiting Officer, Halifax, N.S.*

Author's Note: The above advertisement was published in *"The Atlantic Advocate,"* September, 1916.

First published in The Atlantic Advocate, *September 1916.*
Reprinted courtesy The Atlantic Advocate

York Upper Canada
July 21, 1821

A Black Loyalist

This petition tells the exciting story of Richard Pierpoint, a hero of the time, who was instrumental in the founding of the "Company of Coloured Men."

The Petition of Richard Pierpoint, now of the Town of Niagara, a Man of Colour, a native of Africa, and an inhabitant of this Province since the year 1780.

Most humbly showeth,

That Your Excellency's Petitioner is a native of Bondou in Africa; that at the age of Sixteen Years he was made a Prisoner and sold as a Slave; that he was conveyed to America about the year 1760, and sold to a British officer; that he served his Majesty during the American Revolutionary War in the Corps called Butler's Rangers; and again during the late American War in a Corps of Colour raised on the Niagara Frontier.

That Your Excellency's Petitioner is now old and without property; that he finds it difficult to obtain a livelihood by his labour; that he is above all things desirous to return to his native Country; that His Majesty's Government be graciously pleased to grant him any relief, he wishes it may be by affording him the means to proceed to England and from thence to a Settlement near the Gambia or Senegal Rivers, from whence he could return to Bondou . . .

Reprinted courtesy Headley Tullock, author of Black Canadians: A Long Line of Fighters

NOTES

Introduction

1. C. Bruce Ferguson, *A Documentary Study of the Establishment of the Negroes in Nova Scotia Between the War of 1812 and the Winning of Responsible Government* (Halifax: Public Archives of Nova Scotia, 1948), p. 2.
2. Headley Tullock, *Black Canadians: A Long Line of Fighters* (Toronto: NC Press, 1975), p. 91.
3. Tullock, p. 97.
4. Tullock, p. 97.
5. Tullock, p. 107-108.
6. Ernest Green, "Upper Canada's Black Defenders," *Papers and Records of the Ontario Historical Society*, 27 (1931): 372.
7. Leo W. Bertley, *Canada and Its People of African Descent* (Pierrefonds, Que.: Bilongo Publishers, 1977), p. 67.
8. J. S. Matthews, "British Columbia's First Troops Were Black: 'The Victoria Pioneer Rifle Corps,' 1860," *Army and Navy Veterans in Canada*, Convention Number (1934): 39-40.
9. Dorothy Sterling, *The Making of an Afro-American: Martin Robison Delany, 1812-1885* (New York: Doubleday, 1971), p. 245.
10. Sterling, p. 242.
11. Jim Bearden and Linda Jean Butler, *Shadd: The Life and Times of Mary Shadd Cary* (Toronto: NC Press, 1977), p. 206.
12. Thomas Pakenham, *The Boer War, 1899-1902* (New York: Random House, 1979), p. 418-442. Recent research indicates, however, that the phrase "white man's war" was frequently used during the American Civil War.
13. Department of National Defence, Trump to J. R. B. Whitney, *Records of the Department of National Defence*, 1206, File HQ297-1-21 (Ottawa, March 15, 1916).
14. Department of National Defence, W. G. Gwatkin memorandum (April 13, 1916).

Chapter 1: The Rejection of Black Volunteers

1. Robin Winks, *The Blacks in Canada: A History* (New Haven: Yale University Press, 1971), p. 314.
2. Interview with George Fells (Yarmouth, N.S., September 9, 1982).
3. Barbara Wilson, *Ontario and the First World War, 1914-1918* (Toronto: University of Toronto Press, 1977), p. 108.
4. Department of National Defence, George Morton to Sir Sam Hughes, *Records of the Department of National Defence*, 1206, File HQ297-1-21 (Ottawa, September 7, 1915).
5. Department of National Defence, W. E. Hodgins to T. J. Stewart (October 16, 1915).
6. Department of National Defence, J. F. Tupper to Sir Sam Hughes.
7. Department of National Defence, W. G. Gwatkin to Loring G. Christie (September 30, 1915).
8. Department of National Defence, Beverley R. Armstrong to the Secretary of the Militia Council (November 18, 1915).
9. Department of National Defence, John T. Richards to Sir Sam Hughes (November 21, 1915).
10. Richards to Hughes.
11. Department of National Defence, George W. Fowler to the Acting Adjutant-General, 6th Division, Halifax (November 25, 1915).
12. Department of National Defence, Sir Sam Hughes to John T. Richards (November 25, 1915).
13. Department of National Defence, W. E. Hodgins to the General Officer, 6th Division, Halifax (November 29, 1915).
14. Winks, *The Blacks in Canada*, p. 315.

15. Wilson, *Ontario and the First World War*, p. 108-109.
16. Department of National Defence, J. R. B. Whitney to Sir Sam Hughes (April 18, 1916).
17. Whitney to Hughes.
18. Canada, House of Commons, *Debates*, March 24, 1916, p. 2114-2115.
19. House of Commons, *Debates*, p. 2114-2115.
20. Department of National Defence, Colonel Ogilvie to the Secretary of the Militia Council (December 9, 1915).
21. Ogilvie to the Secretary of the Militia Council.
22. Department of National Defence, W. G. Gwatkin to the adjutant-generals (December 22, 1915).
23. Department of National Defence, E. A. Cruikshank to the Secretary of the Militia Council (March 11, 1916).
24. Department of National Defence, W. G. Gwatkin memorandum (April 13, 1916).
25. Department of National Defence, British War Office to the Governor-General (May 11, 1916).

Chapter 2: No. 2 Construction Battalion, CEF
1. Department of National Defence, "War Diary," *Records of the Department of National Defence* (Ottawa, May 17, 1917).
2. Irving J. Sloan, *Blacks in America, 1492-1970* (Dobbs Ferry, N.Y.: Oceana Publications, 1971), p. 26.
3. Department of National Defence, W. E. Hodgins to Daniel Hugh Sutherland, *Records of the Department of National Defence*, 4558, File HQ132-11-1 (Ottawa, July 31, 1916).
4. Interview with Patricia McGuire (River John, N.S., September 30, 1984).
5. Interview with George McCullion (Pictou, N.S., September 30, 1984).
6. Department of National Defence, Daniel Hugh Sutherland to the DAA and QMG, Military District 6, Halifax, File HQ132-11-1 (August 26, 1916).
7. Leo W. Bertley, *Canada and Its People of African Descent* (Pierrefonds, Que.: Bilongo Publishers, 1977), p. 71.
8. Department of National Defence, Daniel Hugh Sutherland to the Secretary of the Militia Council, *Records of the Department of National Defence*, 1550, File HQ683-124-2 (Ottawa, November 27, 1917).
9. Pierre Berton, *The Promised Land: Settling the West, 1896-1914* (Toronto: McClelland and Stewart, 1984), p. 186.
10. Department of National Defence, "War Diary," (May 17, 1917).
11. Interview with Hilda Lambert (Halifax, N.S., August 8, 1984).
12. Interview with Edith Colley (Dartmouth, N.S., April 7, 1984).
13. Interview with Mabel Saunders (East Preston, N.S., July 14, 1984).
14. Mabel Saunders.

Chapter 3: 106th Battalion, CEF
1. Department of National Defence, W. H. Allen to the DAA and QMG, 6th Division, Halifax, *Records of the Department of National Defence*, 4558, File HQ132-11-1 (Ottawa, December 14, 1915).
2. W. H. Allen to the DAA and QMG, 6th Division.
3. W. H. Allen to the DAA and QMG, 6th Division.
4. W. H. Allen to the DAA and QMG, 6th Division.
5. Interview with Sydney Morgan Jones (Halifax, N.S., March 9, 1985).
6. Interview with Frank Ash (Halifax, N.S., August 11, 1984).

Chapter 4: Conscription
1. Interview with Hilda Lambert (Halifax, N.S., August 3, 1984).
2. Interview with John Crawley (North Preston, N.S., August 10, 1984).
3. Interview with Isaac Phills (Dartmouth, N.S., August 10, 1981).
4. Isaac Phills.

Chapter 6: Reunion and Recognition
1. "Black Veterans Meet," *The Mail-Star* [Halifax], November 13, 1982.

Synopsis
1. Interview with Sydney Morgan Jones (Halifax, N.S., October 4, 1982).
2. A. Fortescue Duguid, *History of the Canadian Forces, 1914-19*, General Series: 1 (Ottawa, 1938), p. 52.
3. Fred Gaffen, *Forgotten Soldiers* (Penticton, B.C.: Theytus Books, 1985).
4. Interview with Gordon Charles Wilson (Halifax, N.S., July 5, 1982).

5. Examples of segregated graveyards are Camp Hill Cemetery, Halifax, N.S., and the Robie Street Cemetery, Truro, N.S.
6. Interview with Lee Carvery (Dartmouth, N.S., September 4, 1984).
7. Interview with Allan Bundy (Dartmouth, N.S., August 30, 1984).

Epilogue

1. Story, Alan, "Battalion of Blacks Honored at Last," *The Star* [Toronto], November 14, 1982.
2. A. Seymour Tyler, Speech, Reunion and Recognition Banquet (Halifax, N.S., November 12, 1982).
3. Edmund Morris, Speech, Reunion and Recognition Banquet (Halifax, N.S., November 12, 1982).

BIBLIOGRAPHY

Bearden, Jim, and Linda Jean Butler. *Shadd: The Life and Times of Mary Shadd Cary*. Toronto: NC Press, 1977.

Bennett, Lerone Jr. *The Shaping of Black America*. Chicago: Johnson Publishing Company, 1975.

Bertley, Leo W. *Canada and Its People of African Descent*. Pierrefonds, Que.: Bilongo Publishers, 1977.

Berton, Pierre. *The Promised Land: Settling the West, 1896-1914*. Toronto: McClelland and Stewart, 1984.

"Black Veterans Meet." *The Mail-Star*. Halifax, November 13, 1982.

Brooks, Thomas R. *Walls Come Tumbling Down: A History of the Civil Rights Movement, 1940-1970*. Englewood Cliffs: Prentice-Hall, 1974.

Canada. Department of National Defence. *Records of the Department of National Defence*, 1206; 1550; 4558; "War Diary," Ottawa, 1915-1917.

Canada. Department of Trade and Commerce. *Canada Year Book, 1916-1917*. Ottawa, 1917.

Canada. House of Commons. *Debates*, March 24, 1916.

Duguid, A. Fortescue. *History of the Canadian Forces, 1914-19*. General Series: 1. Ottawa, 1938.

Ferguson, C. Bruce. *A Documentary Study of the Establishment of the Negroes in Nova Scotia Between the War of 1812 and the Winning of Responsible Government*. Halifax: Public Archives of Nova Scotia, 1948.

Ferguson, Ted. *A White Man's Country*. Toronto: Doubleday Canada, 1975.

Gaffen, Fred. *Forgotten Soldiers*. Penticton, B.C.: Theytus Books, 1985.

Grant, John. *Black Nova Scotians*. Halifax: Nova Scotia Museum, 1980.

Green, Ernest. "Upper Canada's Black Defenders." *Papers and Records of the Ontario Historical Society*, 27 (1931): 365-391.

Henry, Frances. *Forgotten Canadians: The Blacks of Nova Scotia*. Don Mills, Ont.: Longmans Canada, 1973.

Hewlitt, Alexander. *Conscription*. Toronto: Maclean-Hunter Learning Materials, 1972.

Hill, Daniel G. *The Freedom Seekers: Blacks in Early Canada*. Agincourt, Ont.: Book Society of Canada, 1981.

Hostesses of Union United Church. *Memory Book*. Montreal: Union United Church, 1982.

Hunt, Stewart M. *Nova Scotia's Part in the Great War*. Halifax: Nova Scotia Veteran Publishing, 1920.

Jackman, S. W. "The Victoria Pioneer Rifle Corps: British Columbia, 1860-1866." *Journal One of the Society for Army Historical Research*, 39 (March 1961).

Lee, Irvin H. *Negro Medal of Honor Men*. New York: Dodd Mead, 1967.

Machum, George C. *Canada's V.C.s*. Toronto: McClelland and Stewart, 1956.

McPherson, James M. *Marching Toward Freedom: The Negro in the Civil War, 1861-1865*. New York: Alfred A. Knopf, 1965.

Matthews, J. S. "British Columbia's First Troops Were Black: 'The Victoria Pioneer Rifle Corps,' 1860." *Army and Navy Veterans in Canada*, Convention Number (1934).

Morton, Desmond. *A Military History of Canada*. Edmonton: Hurtig, 1985.

—. *A Peculiar Kind of Politics: Canada's Overseas Ministry in the First World War*. Toronto: University of Toronto Press, 1982.

Nova Scotia. Nova Scotia Human Rights Commission. *Pictorial on Black History*. Halifax, 1974.

Pakenham, Thomas. *The Boer War, 1899-1902*. New York: Random House, 1979.

Shermer, David. *World War One*. London: Octopus Books, 1973.

Sloan, Irving J. *Blacks in America, 1492-1970*. Dobbs Ferry, N.Y.: Oceana Publications, 1971.

Smith, T. Watson. "The Slave in Canada." *Collections of the Nova Scotia Historical Society*, 10 (1899).

Spray, W. A. *The Blacks in New Brunswick*. Fredericton: Brunswick Press, 1972.

Sterling, Dorothy. *The Making of an Afro-American: Martin Robison Delany, 1812-1885*. New York: Doubleday, 1971.

Story, Alan. "Battalion of Blacks Honored at Last." *The Star*. Toronto, November 14, 1982.

Thomson, Colin A. *Blacks in Deep Snow: Black Pioneers in Canada*. Don Mills, Ont: J. M. Dent & Sons, 1979.

Tullock, Headley. *Black Canadians: A Long Line of Fighters*. Toronto: NC Press, 1975.

Wakin, Edward. *Black Fighting Men in U.S. History*. New York: Lothrop, Lee & Shepard, 1971.

Walker, James W. *The Black Loyalists: The Search for a Promised Land in Nova Scotia and Sierra Leone, 1783-1878*. New York: Africana Publishing, 1976.

Wesley, Charles, H. *The Quest for Equality*. New York: Publishers Company, 1968.

Wilson, Barbara. *Ontario and the First World War, 1914-1918*. Toronto: University of Toronto Press, 1977.

Winks, Robin. *The Blacks in Canada: A History*. New Haven: Yale University Press, 1971.

ACKNOWLEDGEMENTS

Any work, regardless of its magnitude or scope, owes its existence to the goodwill, co-operation, encouragement and assistance of several individuals and organizations. This book is no exception. I am indebted to many people, too numerous, unfortunately, to mention here.

First of all, a special thanks to the World War I veterans—many now deceased—who provided me with priceless reminiscences. I am also indebted to their widows, relatives and friends who graciously provided photographs and information. In this regard, thanks go to Frederick A. Sparks, Loon Lake, Halifax County, N.S., for twenty photographs of veterans, photographs that his father, John R. Sparks, brought back from Europe; Henry Bishop, the Curator of the Black Cultural Centre for Nova Scotia, who made photographs and information available; Bridgial Pachai, Executive Director of the Black Cultural Centre, for his expert guidance; Clifford Skinner and Raymond Richards, both Saint John, N.B., for photographs of, and information concerning, New Brunswick veterans; Montreal's Thamis Gale for information on surviving veterans in Quebec and Ontario; and David States of the Nova Scotia Human Rights Commission for his research.

I am grateful to the Board of Directors of The Society for the Protection and Preservation of Black Culture in Nova Scotia for entrusting me with the original undertaking. I am also grateful to George F. McCurdy, the former director of the Nova Scotia Human Rights Commission, and my good friends Phyllis and Gordon Lucas for their constant encouragement.

Bruce Ellis, the Curator of the Army Museum, Halifax Citadel, provided extremely helpful editorial guidance. Captain George Borden, Canadian Armed Forces, Halifax, passed on useful information and suggestions, as did Halifax reporter Alex E. Nickerson. I am also indebted to Major Robert Maxwell, Canadian Armed Forces, Ottawa, for his dedicated assistance, support and interest.

Many thanks, as well, to the staffs of the Public Archives of Nova Scotia, the Public Archives of Canada and the Dartmouth Regional Library for their assistance.

Thanks are due to my brother Arthur for his invaluable production expertise. Judi Mason and Cheryl Byard, Maritime School of Social Work, and Maxine Brooks, the Black Cultural Centre, generously typed portions of the manuscript.

I am grateful to the various Royal Canadian Legion branches, veteran's organizations, church and secular groups, businesses and individuals who provided moral and financial support. Their generosity made the Reunion and Recognition Weekend in November 1982 a tremendous success. The weekend, in turn, furnished the motivation for this modest work. I must not forget my wife, Joyce, who was a tower of strength and support throughout this labour of love. She was my constant companion on my numerous trips around the province. Her patience and understanding made this journey into the past an unforgettable and enjoyable experience.

Most of all, I humbly give heartfelt thanks to our Lord and Saviour for his gifts of love, health, strength, interest and desire, which enabled me to persevere.

I have made every effort to obtain permission to reprint and quote and to acknowledge all sources of information. I alone, however, am responsible for any shortcomings this book may have.

Calvin W. Ruck, RSW
September 8, 1987

PHOTO CREDITS

INDEX